Freedom by a Hair's Breadth

Tsimihety in Madagascar

Peter J. Wilson

Ann Arbor

THE UNIVERSITY OF MICHIGAN PRESS

Copyright © by the University of Michigan 1992
All rights reserved
Published in the United States of America by
The University of Michigan Press
Manufactured in the United States of America

1995   1994   1993   1992   4   3   2   1

Library of Congress Cataloging-in-Publication Data

Wilson, Peter J.
    Freedom by a hair's breadth : Tsimihety in Madagascar / Peter J.
Wilson.
        p.   cm.
    Includes bibliographical references and index.
    ISBN 0-472-10389-X (alk. paper)
    1. Tsimihety (Malagasy people) 2. Tsimihety (Malagasy people—
Ethnic identity. 3. Tsimihety (Malagasy people)—Politics and
government. I. Title.
DT469.M277T788   1992
305.89'93—dc20   92-28344
                                                            CIP

To the memory of my father, William M. Wilson
June 19, 1903 – Feb. 20, 1992

Izay manoro lalana mahitsy, mamindra aina

Acknowledgments

My first and foremost debt must go to Donald and Jean Schofield, then of the London Missionary Society, now happily more or less retired in Bromley. Donald knows far more about Tsimihety than anyone else, Tsimihety included, and I put this effort before him with due humility. But, on behalf of my wife Joan as well, I want to acknowledge a debt of friendship that gave us great pleasure. Great kindness and fellowship were also shown us by Graeme and Ella Smith at the Mandritsara Station, and by John Gilbey in Tananarive. Over the years I have discussed Tsimihety with several fellow travelers, and for their stimulus I must mention with gratitude Gillian Feeley-Harnik and Aidan Southall. I have had numerous stabs at writing this book, but the final and successful push was made possible by a sabbatical leave from the University of Otago, to whom I express my appreciation, particularly to Assistant Vice Chancellor David McKenzie and fellow members of my department. I am grateful to Joyce Harrison, of the University of Michigan Press. Finally, the research in Androna was made possible by Grant G-24143 from the National Science Foundation.

Preface

The discovery, or invention, of the ideal of personal liberty is usually claimed by European political philosophy. And then it is argued it has been a recent discovery. Isaiah Berlin did not think the Ancient Greeks had a conscious sense of freedom, so doubtless he would not accord such a sense to obscure, nonliterate, and non-European people living in isolated corners of the earth. European and American trained administrators and executives, brought up to think they were bringing freedom (and democracy) to an enslaved world, have all too often been mystified by the extent and the vehemence of the opposition shown to their efforts. And this opposition has purported to be in the very name of that freedom that the West thought it was introducing for the first time. In the past anthropologists have not helped the understanding of this puzzle by calling upon Durkheimian sociological theory to explain their findings. The Durkheimian thesis emphasizes the reclamation of social institutions by identifying their constraining functions and effects and underplaying their enabling properties. The "logic of the system," explained at the social and matching symbolic level, all too often suggests people living as if in the midst of a clockwork world, their options not just limited but obliterated in favor of prescriptions and postscriptions. It is not that there are no rules and taboos in such societies, there surely are. But what is not perceived so clearly is that the rules, the symbols, the customs, and the ways of doing things are themselves the outcome of choices, and they are choices that continue to be made, and varied, according to changing conditions. Such a view has been recently formulated and designated as *structuration* by Anthony Giddens (1984).

With very few exceptions, in fact probably none at all, there exists no community of people without neighbors. Even the isolated island communities of the Pacific have always been in touch with each other. The supposedly isolated bands of gatherer/hunters seem mostly to have lived in contact with sedentary neighbors. It is well known that most names used by ethnographers to designate "tribes" are in fact not names but general designations meaning "the people." But, "we the people" reflects not uniqueness so much as the attempt to define the superiority of oneself over neighbors (the "Nuer" versus the "Dinka," or "We, the Tikopia"). Dislike and disgust of "other" people is a far more widespread and deep-seated phenomenon than Western liberal feeling is likely to admit, though Freud warned us this was so. As well as the contact between neighbors, the ethnographic world has also, in the past four hundred years, been affected by the colonizing activities of European nations and their cultures. This separation with contact indicates an ongoing exposure of people to each other and is expressed in numerous "borrowings" and rejections, adoptions, and resistances—that is in the continuing exercise of choices by individuals and groups. To varying degrees, then, there are no untouched indigenous societies that have developed their ways of life without any consideration of, and influence from, neighbors, outsiders, conquerors, colonizers, trading partners, missionaries, and many, many more.

People in non-Western cultures may be free to choose, but this may so be taken for granted that the idea of what they are doing, its presence as a principle, may not be evident to them, and so, as Isaiah Berlin argues, freedom may not be a central value or principle of action and thought. I would take this to be the case in Madagascar for the people who came to call themselves (and be called) Tsimihety. I shall therefore try to identify the circumstances in which "freedom" was brought to the surface by events that negated freedom before the idea of freedom was known to Tsimihety. With the invasion of the Merina their undefined situation was suddenly defined as an unfree one, and freedom, or at least its conditions, were invented (or discovered). The confrontation between freedom and unfreedom is, then, acted out as resistance. These circumstances of a foreign presence, which was often oppressive, helped to focus Tsimihety attention on freedom as a goal and hence on whatever endeavors might contribute to realizing those social, cultural, and economic conditions that would make freedom possible. I would concur with Joseph Raz that, of these conditions, the fundamental one is autonomy, that condition by which the individual is sufficiently independent in a material and social sense to be at least a part creator of his or her own moral world (Raz 1986:154–55).

The conditions for freedom among the Tsimihety must, a priori, differ from the conditions of liberty in a modern capitalist society. In a democratic free-market society the foundation of freedom is the condition by which each individual has the opportunity to buy or sell without hindrance. The achievement of such freedom is measured largely in monetary terms—that individual is free who enjoys the unhampered opportunity to improve his well-being by his own efforts at buying and selling, especially his labor power. However, Tsimihety perceived the use of money in "free" exchange to be a major step toward dependency on outsiders and, at least until 1963, they made only minimal use of money. Their conditions of freedom must, therefore, be upheld by a different framework. It is this framework I shall endeavor to describe in this book. Fundamentally I shall argue that conventional cultural institutions common in some form or other throughout Madagascar were utilized by Tsimihety to resist domination from the outside.

There is little evidence that the Merina conquest of much of Madagascar had the same sort of benevolent intentions as French colonization. Both Merina and French, of course, had their own self-interests uppermost. But the French, heirs to the most action-packed expression of liberty in Europe, had intentions to "civilize." In Androna they sought to diversify the crops of the region; they tried to turn pastoralism into an economic activity by establishing a meat processing works south of Androna, in Antsihanaka; they furthered enlightenment by encouraging both Protestants and Catholics to missionize; they tried to develop literacy by backing schools; and they brought in modern medicine by establishing a small hospital in Mandritsara. By establishing industry and exports, a bureaucracy, a civil service, and by encouraging commerce, the French could well be said to have vastly expanded the range of options from which individuals could choose in order to achieve personal fulfillment and self-realization. Though there may have been the equal intention to further French ends, there can be no doubt that, in terms of any theory of personal liberty, the conditions for such liberty were greatly expanded by the French. But most Tsimihety rejected both the French and the options, as indeed many indigenous people elsewhere in the world have rejected Western values. That the French did expand the conditions of Tsimihety freedom in the eyes of some is made evident by the fact that some Tsimihety did choose to become educated, to become professionals and government ministers. The first president of the Republic, Philibert Tsiranana, was first a schoolmaster, then a politician. But most people rejected French values and French-made opportunities, and in the eyes of most of the Europeans I met, this rejection was more or less incomprehensible. The Tsimihety were being offered evolution, progress, wealth, and relief from enslavement to antiquated customs. Why did they remain so conservative?

One part of the answer to this question was that Tsimihety remained suspicious of all outsiders, no matter what their intentions. In part this no doubt reflected fear, but in part it also reflected the desire to remain independent. This independence included the capacity to define one's own goals and methods of achieving them, again what Raz calls the control over one's own moral world. Options originating from the outside, but that remain governed externally, are not so much an expansion of the conditions of freedom as they are a multiplication of the restraints on freedom, as well as an expansion of their range. Tsimihety may have been able to choose to become functionaries, but in so doing they put themselves in direct subjection to a colonial, or external, government. It was best, then, that Tsimihety lived in a limited world over which they had control and which gave them autonomy, rather than in an enlarged world in which autonomy could not be maintained. Hence, I argue for their employment of "traditional" institutions as conditions for autonomy and freedom. However, when national independence is understood as a state of autonomy for Tsimihety by Tsimihety I would expect their outlook to change. They would begin to modernize.

Contents

Introduction

The fieldwork on which this study is based was carried out more than twenty-eight years ago. My wife, Joan, and I spent eleven months in Madagascar, nine of those with Tsimihety. For getting to know Tsimihety people intimately it was woefully inadequate. It was not even sufficient to achieve a reasonable fluency in the Tsimihety regional dialect of Malagasy, and so my relations with individual Tsimihety were always at risk of stumbling against the first barrier, language. What made life even more difficult was the fact that many individuals sometimes went out of their way to exaggerate their rustic accent, to speak extremely rapidly, and to use archaic words and elaborate syntax, partly to confuse me because I was an outsider and partly to entertain one another at my expense. Not only was I an outsider and a European, but also in the beginning the hesitant Malagasy I did speak was based on the Merina dialect, which I had learned in America from tapes. Though I was fortunate in getting the services of an assistant cum translator, Tsimanefa (a pseudonym), not too long after my arrival in Mandritsara, there was no doubt where his loyalties lay, and I certainly cannot blame him for monitoring both my questions and respondents' answers through his translations. After six months or so I knew enough Malagasy and was familiar enough with the regional dialect to be able to appreciate what was going on. I was frustrated, of course, but it never crossed my mind at the time that Tsimihety people had good reasons for not wanting me to find out too much and that they may not have wanted a too intimate acquaintance. I had supposed, like most anthropologists, that my study, being of scientific intent, was absolutely neutral and disinterested, and I expected those I wished to study to view it as equally harmless and nonthreatening.

We also experienced great difficulty in trying to live permanently in a Tsimihety village. Strangers, whoever they may be, were not overtly welcome and, while hospitality was always provided, strangers were expected to move on in a day or so. Our requests to set up house in a village were consistently turned down. Looking back I can understand now that the difficulties Tsimihety people put in the way of our attempts to live with them in a village were part of the larger political problem with which they had to live. It is true that, although most of them were familiar with white men, they knew them only at a distance and in an impersonal capacity as officials or traders. Missionaries had tried to become more intimate but had succeeded with only a few individuals. White women were known to exist but were certainly unknown as real people. They were an invisible presence only. So, our requests for permanent accommodation were strange and unprecedented. But what I now think was even more puzzling and threatening was that here we were, strangers (*vazaha*) and Europeans apparently bent on trying to become Tsimihety. Strangers in general were feared among the Tsimihety, but here we were white strangers (a rarity) requesting *permanent* abode (quite unheard of). It was not that individuals were unfriendly or hostile, it was mostly that we unwittingly belonged to a category (stranger) about which Tsimihety were unusually sensitive, and to a sub-category (white stranger) about which they had great misgivings. It was also distinctly odd that white people should wish to live in the villages and not in Mandritsara, the district capital where the white population was traditionally concentrated. It was only after several months of persistence and growing familiarity that we were able, through the good offices of Tsimanefa, to live in our own house in the village of Ankiabe Salohy. Unfortunately after about two months we received news of my mother-in-law's terminal illness and decided to return to the United States.

Prior to that I visited the villages of Andilamena and Ambandriky on a daily basis. These villages were a few kilometers from the mission station and increasingly I was able to visit among people there without an interpreter. Shortly before his death, Velo, the *mpijoro* or ritual head of the village, adopted me as his grandson and I enjoyed a sort of Tsimihety identity. But although there was some intimacy and informality it was not very great.

These circumstances of my fieldwork are important in many respects. Obviously I never got anywhere near immersion in Tsimihety culture, nor did I ever get to the point where I had to, or could, think as a Tsimihety in Tsimihety situations. There is no way I could write an ethnography that reported on my transposition from inside one culture to another (and back again) which provided an authoritative account and analysis of the Tsimihety taken from within the culture and explained it in its own terms and categories. For many years this failure has inhibited my attempts to "write up" my data. And, as the years went by and I was occupied with other projects and interests, my data and my memories of my experiences among the Tsimihety grew more and more distant. An obvious solution was to return for further fieldwork, but the chance came to do fieldwork in Malaysia soon afterward and then a combination of personal and political circumstances made fieldwork in Madagascar inadvisable. Furthermore, given the desire for political privacy that dominated Tsimihety, I became increasingly beset by doubts about the propriety of further fieldwork with them—perhaps I should mind my own business and leave them to theirs. However, the longer I delayed any moves to return, the more the data I had was becoming less and less fresh until I realized that it was, in fact, becoming history, in which case new fieldwork could no longer continue the earlier work; it would have to be new work. I do not know the exact point at which I realized my Tsimihety fieldwork was history, but it was at that point that it occurred to me that the difficulties of exclusion which the Tsimihety had imposed on me were not unique or coincidental. They could very well have been an active part of the wider situation that enveloped the Tsimihety and which they regarded as a, if not the, major problem and purpose of their political existence. I was not a neutral and detached scientific observer to Tsimihety people; I was yet another part of an ongoing problem with which their lives were confronted. This was the problem of outside interference, or even just outside presence. If this was the case, then I was part of the problem and my fieldwork was a firsthand experience of the constitution of this problem.

My circumstances are no doubt extreme, but I suggest that the extremity of this case throws into relief a wider and deeper ethnographic problem that pervades all anthropology. I shall call it the problem of distance. The problem of distance has many sides, the most important of which may be specified as follows.

Although there are some exceptions, anthropologists have invariably chosen to study "underdogs." These include "tribes" living in marginal environments of a state, such as Amazonian tribes or North American Indians; tribal people living under a newly established colonial regime, such as most British ethnographic studies in Africa represent; the poor, slum dwellers of large metropolises or the rural peasantry, descriptions of which fill the library shelves of Latin American anthropology. The anthropologist is rarely either a tribal person, a slum dweller, a peasant, or, for that matter, one who has been colonized. There are some who fit these categories, but they are still exceptional. Most anthropologists are white, middle-class, urban dwellers by origin, if not by sympathy, and they come from Europe or the United States. They are outsiders, but not just neutral outsiders. They are in the same general category of outsider as those who represent, exercise, and administer the domination of a colonial or postcolonial economic master, or who insist on the development of those they are pleased to regard as underdeveloped, or even undeveloped. However much they may disown such an identification by word and deed there must always be the suspicion that their relationship with the subjects of their studies is shaded by their original associations. As outsiders, they experience the ways in which those on the margins deal with those of the center and hence with the problem of their political distance. Do those on the margins aspire to the center? Do they admire it and wish to emulate it? Or do they despise the center? Do they oppose it? Do they do everything possible to neutralize their relationship? Do they strive to merge? To cut themselves off? In other words, the ready acceptance or rejection of the anthropologist, and his or her enjoyment of intimacy and help, is possibly symptomatic of a wider relationship and people's perception of it. I suspect that this element of distance is often minimized in order to convince the reader of an ethnography that the report, description, and analysis is as authentic as possible (leaving aside problems of cultural translation and the philosophical problem of getting to know the "other"). How close one person can get to another is a contentious philosophical as well as a practical issue. Often, an individual thinks he or she has successfully lost one identity and gained another, but that person's original identity is rarely forgotten: among the Tsimihety, for example, people from other ethnic groups who have married Tsimihety often have had their foreignness remembered and their children's alien parentage brought up if the occasion demanded. I am therefore skeptical of any claims by anthropologists to have "become" another person. They may, however, have been accepted, not as a tribal person, but as an anthropologist or friend of the people, a surprising exception to the usual white person who is made, temporarily, an honorary tribal person. When this acceptance occurs I think the important thing about it is that the people being studied accept the distance between them and the anthropologist; the fact that the anthropologist is *studying* others indicates this distance. The innermost perceptions of the member of one culture can never vanish to be replaced by those of another; they always remain distant. I take it as proof of this that the anthropologist could never write a book or a paper if her or she really had gotten inside "other" people. The act of writing presupposes the distanced stance. In the case of the present book, it is written from almost the outermost perimeter.

For reasons that will become apparent, there was, for Tsimihety, a distinct line between themselves and all others. They were at the center, but those outside the center were at varying distances depending on the similarity of political experience. Closest were people like the Betsimisaraka and Sakalava, who were not only neighbors but also people known to be similarly affected by Merina conquest and French colonialism. People like the Betsimisaraka and Sakalava were also close because in some senses they were ancestral to Tsimihety. At the next level of distance came other Malagasy such as Betsileo, Antandroy, Bara, and Makoa. Such people were from distant parts of Madagascar and they played little, if any, part in Tsimihety history. Such people were accepted as settlers in the region, but they lived in their own villages and rarely as household neighbors in Tsimihety villages. The next ring comprised Merina. The Merina were the most distant of all Malagasy people as far as Tsimihety were concerned, for the simple reason that in the past the Merina tried to dominate Tsimihety by force and administrative dominance and, in 1963, they were the dominant people of Madagascar. Merina, too, lived among Tsimihety but only those descended from slaves (*Hova mainty*) had been allowed to found their own villages and had been granted land by Tsimihety. Finally, the outermost circle of Tsimihety acquaintance consisted of Europeans—people of another culture, another land, and another race. On these grounds alone it was virtually inconceivable that Europeans could be incorporated into Tsimihety life. But when Europeans had also been a politically dominant force that had tried to exploit and rule Tsimihety, then even acceptance into Tsimihety life was hard to imagine. This distanced the anthropologist as far as Tsimihety were concerned, and a great deal of my fieldwork was concerned with trying to move through the barriers closer to the center. It was not that as separate individuals some Tsimihety were not friendly. They were, and both Joan and myself enjoyed many spontaneous occasions of fun, humor, sadness, and work. But these never jelled into close relationships, or relationships beyond relaxed friendship. But the very spontaneity of such engagements was incompatible with serious ethnographic inquiry. For example, during the spontaneous intimacy of a casual meal, I might ask why the woman brought the food into the house on her knees when there were guests. The answer I would get would be, "That is the Tsimihety way" (*fomba Tsimihety*). I might know full well that there was more to it than that, but to confirm this I should not turn the sociability of the occasion into a serious interview. To find out more meant waiting to arrange a more focused interview. To make such an arrangement was what proved difficult—it made people suspicious and returned me to the outer circle. If, however, discussions about such conduct as meal serving could be provoked during spontaneous occasions I would get my deeper information and still remain close to the inner circle.

All anthropologists record their experience—on tape, film, or laptop computers perhaps—but invariably and to the greatest extent in fieldnotes. (My fieldnotes are entirely written as I had no tape recorder. I have a few, black-and-white photos only, because my 35mm camera was shattered on a rock.) Some even take time out from their immediate fieldwork to fill out their notebooks free from interruption. Daily life in a village does not make provision for extensive note-taking, and the very fact that every anthropologist has to make notes, no matter how close he or she claims to get to those being studied, retains that distance and externality.

No anthropologist, as far as I know, publishes fieldnotes, tapes, or film without some sort of editing. Most published ethnography is a "writing up" of fieldnotes, which means a writing beyond what the fieldnotes actually say. But even if there was no writing beyond, the fact remains that it is fieldnotes, the written record of events and experiences, that are the actual data reported either directly (quotations) or indirectly. Ethnography is based on documents, and these documents are, because they are hurriedly written, a selective representation of experience. Later "writing up" augments fieldnotes by invoking memories and felt reconstructions, but these are inevitably distanced from the event. I am arguing here that although ethnography claims to be firsthand and therefore different from history, in fact this claim does not mean much. I will press the point with my own, extreme example. My fieldnotes are twenty-eight years old. I say "my" fieldnotes but the "I" who wrote this chapter in 1989 is a changed person from the "I" of twenty-eight years ago who scribbled the fieldnotes. The situation differs only in degree from the normal. Thus, most published ethnographies are rewrites of Ph.D. theses, and the writing both of thesis and monograph takes place back in the country of origin, removed from the fieldwork situation, and uses field-notes as the data. The writing process may take several years, and thus the temporal as well as the spatial distance increases. The returned anthropologist must rejoin his own society and the specialized sector of it, which becomes his audience and judge. He must often do this imme-diately if he wants to get the Ph.D. and then a job and so, even if he "became" an "other" in the field, when he writes his report he must quickly revert back to his own "self." Unless I am quite mistaken, I have a hunch that most of the serious questioning about cultural dif-ference and self-identity that many anthropologists enter into occurs at this time of disengagement from the "other" and after the return home. In the field the anthropologist may be totally overwhelmed and so uncom-fortable and ill at ease that he or she does not question, because to do so increases detachment and solitude, the two nightmares of fieldwork. This often leads to self-pity; one simply wants to get out. Or, the anthro-pologist may be striving so hard to assimilate that there is no time for questioning because such questioning impedes assimilation.

In my situation among the Tsimihety, as I have indicated, I never got "inside," and most of my fieldnotes are derived from observation rather than participation. I did participate in household and village life, in rituals, and in subsistence activities, but I could not claim to have *experienced* insider feelings. I never buried my own flesh and blood, nor did I see any of my descendants born; I did not have to search out a wife, or prove myself by cattle rustling; I never had to decide whether to move elsewhere for better pasture or rice fields; I never had to make the sorts of decisions that every Tsimihety has to make as the stuff of life because my life never really depended on such decisions. My eth-nographic experience was an interlude in my life, and however intense it might have been for a short period, its events could never be as real and as permanent as they were for Tsimihety. I was lucky in that neither I nor Joan fell ill and had to consult Tsimihety medicine. I never had to take evasive action from government officials. What I was most con-scious of, then as now, was the distance between myself and the Tsimihety I met and came to know. It was a distance that I thought I was trying to narrow, but which I felt they were always trying to maintain toward me, not as the individual who some of them became friendly with, but as the questioner, the observer, the white, alien quasi-official. This could have easily led to a certain paranoia on my part, but I see from my notes that although I felt frustrated and even annoyed I was not becoming obsessed by Tsimihety distancing. I tried hard to proclaim my innocence and my nonofficial status. But I discovered from conversations with other Europeans and particularly with two non-Tsimihety Malagasy, one a Merina and the other a Betsileo, that Tsimihety were hard to deal with. Both men were married to Tsimihety wives, but both spoke to me, in general terms, of the standoffishness of the Tsimihety and of their independence. Tsimihety were regarded by other Malagasy as being hard to deal with. One could get along with individual Tsimihety on a person-to-person basis, but not on a role or status basis. Europeans complained of the way in which Tsimihety simply went their own way no matter what they might have promised to do. The hospital doctor felt it was impossible to treat patients because of this. What was the good of prescribing medicines if you could not be sure whether they would be taken? My own situation and identification as an anthropologist was meaningless in its specifics to Tsimihety, but in its generality I was yet another instance of the "outsider" or vazaha, so how I got along with Tsimihety and what transpired between us was illustrative and exemplary of the relationship between the Tsimihety and all other non-Tsimihety–the outside world. More precisely, no matter how much of an individual I was seen to be I was also and always a political presence because all outsiders, and especially white ones, were political presences. My experience, therefore, was representative of the *political* relationship that was ever present between Tsimihety and the outside. This is what provides the perspective for the following account of Tsimihety.

This relationship is absolutely central to the understanding of the life of any people in the modern world. No community exists in isolation, though some may be more cut off than others. Every community, culture, tribe, or society has to be understood, at least in part, by the contexts in which it exists; it is more than just possible that whatever people do and think is addressed to, and takes much of its meaning and motivation from, the relation between itself and its context. As Wittgenstein argues for language, so we might insist that any regular activity takes its meaning from the relation it bears to the context in which it occurs. What people do may be done with at least half an eye to influencing the distance between them and the outside as well as with the intention of managing their private and personal affairs. In fact it can be argued that the very being of private and personal affairs is possible only because they have to be defined out of a context. So the marginal position in which I found myself turns out to be, in hindsight, representative of a, if not the, critical feature of modern Tsimihety life—the context, which is dominated by the political, i.e., the colonial or quasi-colonial. My advantage as an anthropologist was simply that, unlike European doctors, missionaries, teachers, and adminstrators, Indian and Cormorian traders, Merina, and other Malagasy settlers, I had no other job to do and so had the time to observe the Tsimihety more closely and record their doings in this context. Using these fieldnotes as history I am now in a position to be able to relate Tsimihety institutions to the political context from which they took a significant part of their meaning. In more impersonal language we are speaking of social structures and institutions being the products of interaction between sets of people rather than indigenously generated, pure phenomena.

This book, then, is neither a study of Tsimihety society and culture as a thing in itself, nor a study of the activities of the varieties of outsiders who have affected and continue to affect Tsimihety life. It is a study of how the Tsimihety reacted to the context of their lives and, by so doing, contributed to the context of life for other Malagasy and Europeans, particularly those who were in some sort of official administrative or executive contact with them. I was unconsciously part of the outside and the context. They frustrated me as they frustrated administrators (though in a different way of course). As well, I am temporally and spatially distanced as I am working almost entirely from written sources—my fieldnotes, which include copies of administrative documents of which I am not the author. My notes are supplemented, hazily, by memories and by reference to the accounts published by other anthropologists of their work among other Malagasy peoples. I have no tapes and very few photos. In a sense, then, this is not a "realistic" study, by which I mean I do not try to convey the feel of life among the Tsimihety; I do not try to transport the reader to Ankiabe Salohy or to bring individuals to life on the printed page. In a sense, what follows is more fiction than fact, the documentation of a political strategy pursued under specific conditions for the achievement and maintenance of freedom. It seems to me that my fieldnotes make sense—the notes "add up"—if they are understood and interpreted as constituting the evidence for an otherwise incoherent (or inarticulate) policy of independence followed by the Tsimihety. No individual Tsimihety ever told me that the main thing that mattered in his or her life was political liberty, personal freedom, or being left alone by outsiders. But people's actions certainly spoke to this all the time, and conversations among Tsimihety, as well as some speeches at meeting, made this desire for liberty quite explicit. All the records of individual activities, practices, observances, sayings, and discussions in my fieldnotes can be made to hang together if I suggest they are aimed at ensuring Tsimihety autonomy, which they perceived was under threat from the outside. Institutions, customs, acts, and practices are, of course, the foundation of an ethnography and hence are united into a basic social system that is re-presented and reflected in a symbolic system. Institutions are the sources of belief and hence the framework that supports the ethnography. They are the specific applications of general anthropological theory. In this book such a position is almost reversed because the institutions were not so much the framework as the elements supported by a framework of the total political context. I argue that these social institutions were meaningful in a framework of liberty. What I want to bring out is the possibility that institutions such as forms of descent, norms of residence, constants of land tenure, supernatural beliefs and practices, an egalitarian management of local affairs, and preferred economic practices may also be operated as means to political ends, in this particular case, as means to the guardianship of liberty. Such functions may not be the only, the intended, or even the primary functions of these institutions, but I want to suggest that under the conditions of the history and contemporary life of Tsimihety, institutions can be put to uses other than, or in addition to, those specified by orthodox anthropological theory.

My fieldnotes, in their disconnectedness, repetitiveness, and suggestiveness, call desperately for ideas to make something coherent of them. The ideas confronting the notes dart in and out, coming and going, trying to encompass the notes, picking up those that fall out until, eventually I hope, there emerges a unity and a peace between ideas and notes. The transformation of fieldnotes into an organized, sequential, argued book is not the representation of the facts of the matter as they are (or were) but a presentation of a theory of those facts, or rather, the notes. This is a long-established procedure in ethnography, though it is not as widely or as readily recognized as it might be. But as long ago as 1940, Evans-Pritchard admitted that he was not describing the Nuer as they "really" are but as a theory of them suggested they might be:

But in case it might be said that we have only described the facts
in relation to a theory of them as exemplifications of it and have
subordinated description to analysis, we reply that this was our
intention. (Evans-Pritchard 1940:261)

But where does the theory of the facts come from? In the present instance
I think I can recount the series of mental events that led to the realization
that my notes about the Tsimihety were related to the subject of liberty.
I knew from the time I had to leave Madagascar prematurely that my
data were not intimate and detailed enough. I also knew I had been
somewhat frustrated by the stonewalling and evasive tactics of people
when I asked questions. I was all too well aware of Tsimihety feelings
about government (*fanjakana*) and of political tensions in some of the
villages that related to the activities of the Parti Sociale Démocratique
(PSD), some of which were quite inflammatory and about which I possessed knowledge dangerous to myself and to others. I dared not inquire
further. But most important of all, I knew from observation that some
information was simply not to be had. The artistic life of the Tsimihety
was plain and unenthusiastic; their ritual life was matter-of-fact and
virtually unadorned by ceremony; their economic practices and technology were basic and without elaboration, almost purely utilitarian, for
use, not exchange or display; their political life had little structure and
no hierarchy; the majority of people I met and knew were disinterested
in European technology and education and distrustful of money; they
had "clans" but did little with them. And so on. Tsimihety culture was
Spartan and provided little of the exotic material that inspires incredulity
in lay people and out of which anthropologists are challenged to make
sense by formulating an ethnologic. You cannot write about people whose
chief characteristic seems to be that they do not have what every other
tribal people possess. More than anything else this impression, which I
took away from the field and which was reinforced and thrown back at
me everytime I looked at my fieldnotes, was the stimulus that, very
slowly, stirred my mind to come up with ideas, a theory about the notes.
Once it dawned on me that what my notes and sentiments about my
Tsimihety experiences were telling me was that the distance was what
they were all about, the fieldnotes themselves became the clues to understanding the Tsimihety policy of independence:

An inquiry consists in picking out clues as such, that is, with a

presumed bearing on the presence of something they appear to
indicate. (Polanyi 1966:31)

Or, as a somewhat neglected philosopher of history, and many other
disciplines, R. G. Collingwood, observed, the historian only has at his
disposal "relics" and what he must try to do is to understand what these
are relics of and what they were for when they were not relics (1978:109).
Fieldnotes are, on the one hand, relics of fieldwork, but what was the
fieldwork about? Fieldnotes are textual relics of events, actions, conversations, feelings, and observations. What were they when they were
not relics? In the broadest sense I take it they were my reactions to what
I now perceive was the Tsimihety policy of independence, their desire
for liberty.

So, what follows is not a polishing up of my fieldnotes to depict
the life of some insignificant people in an isolated corner of the world.
It is my contemporary attempt to bring to the surface the hidden (hidden
from me in 1963) ideas that guided my recording of fieldnotes reporting
on Tsimihety. Why did I write the fieldnotes I did?

Historical knowledge is the re-enactment in the historian's mind of
the thought whose history he is studying. (Collingwood 1978:112)

Not the thought of the Tsimihety but the relation between their thought
and mine, the fieldworker. Just as the life of Tsimihety, even if it was
preoccupied with freedom, cannot be considered apart from the context
that constrained that freedom at the same time as it defined it, so no
anthropological account can be other than an account of the relationship
between the object of study and the researcher. It just so happens that,
in the present instance, my own slowness and dimness has magnified
this issue to visibility where otherwise it might have remained micro-
scopic.

I argue in chapter 1 that the likely reason for Tsimihety search for
freedom is to be found in the circumstances of the history of the region
over the past 160 years. I imply that the state of Tsimihety "structure"
was but part of a flow of institutional adaptation, much as the present
is part of the flow of history. Chapter 2 discusses the material conditions
of Tsimihety life, the way in which they managed the necessities. It ana-
lyzes in particular the organization of the allocation of those materials.
In chapter 3 I discuss further aspects of allocation, but concentrate

mostly on the social organization of political and economic decision making, or how egalitarianism was pursued and maintained. Chapter 4 is concerned with a traditional anthropological subject, kinship, but my emphasis is less traditional. I single out the enabling rather than the constraining aspects of kinship and ascent. In chapter 5 I deal, as far as I am able, with questions of the distribution of power and decision making that arose out of the confrontation of necessity with ideals. Tsimihety was part and parcel of Malagasy culture, and Malagasy culture has hierarchy built into it. Everyday situations were sometimes fraught with uncertainty and anxiety (illness for instance), and their resolution could often result in the establishment of authority, if not power. How is egalité reconciled with "power"? I conclude that Tsimihety freedom was not, as first appeared, the desire for freedom from outside determination, but the desire to be free to choose—among other things, whether to link up with the outside or not.

CHAPTER 1

Reconstruction

On arriving in Tananarive, the capital of the Republic of Madagascar, we began the process of visiting officials and fellow academics and anyone who might help us decide where to carry out our ethnographic study. I had one general condition—to be able to work in adjacent areas with different ecologies with a view to studying possible correlations between ecology and social organization. Several people mentioned Tsimihety and gave as their reason that very little was known about them. This was surprising in view of the fact that the first president of the new republic was Tsimihety from the region of Androna. No doubt it was his coming to national power that sparked an interest in Tsimihety and, at the same time, made it evident to other Malagasy that they knew little about them. It was, however, difficult to get to Tsimihety because the only through road from Tananarive was open only for about three weeks of the year. When we were just about to give up and work somewhere else, word came through that Donald Schofield, a London Missionary Society (LMS) missionary at Mandritsara, was coming down and we could possibly drive back up with him. Schofield was delighted at the idea of company, and we were excited to be taken to work among people about whom little was known elsewhere in Madagascar.

This ignorance of the Tsimihety was not simply a question of urban disdain for provincials, an expression of the tendency of city dwellers to lump together everyone else from the countryside. Tsimihety merited very little space in the various histories and surveys of Madagascar compared to their immediate neighbors, the Sakalava and the Betsimi-saraka. In fact, I could find no mention of Tsimihety before the 1880s, and although sources agreed that their location was in the northeast, the extent of that location was very vague. The information that was available was meager and problematic.

In his *Histoire de Madagascar* (1961), Hubert Deschamps reproduces

15

two ethnic maps. One, based on Grandidier's work in 1908, is termed *ancienne;* the other, *nouvelle,* is dated 1958. In the first map Tsimihety are shown in lowercase, light type, covering about one inch of unbounded space; in the second map Tsimihety is printed in capitals and bold type extending two inches and located in a bounded space. In the second map Tsimihety have taken up some of the space occupied by the Sakalava in the earlier map. As I shall discuss, Grandidier's identification of the Tsinihety reflects doubts as to whether they were an ethnic group in the same sense as the Sakalava or the Betsimisaraka were considered to be at the time. In 1905 André You estimated there were 35,000 Tsimihety, while, writing in 1931, Grandidier estimated about 45,000 Tsimihety in the early years of the century (Grandidier 1931:308). Approximately fifty years later, in 1958, Grandidier gave the contemporary population of the Tsimihety as 349,500, and Thompson and Adloff (1965) suggest 363,897. This, if accurate, represents a tenfold increase in fifty years, quite remarkable by any standards. In fifty years Tsimihety had gone from being demographically insignificant to making up almost a twelfth of the nation. In a short space of time, Tsimihety had gone from being barely recognized as an ethnic group to being classified as one of Madagascar's major ethnic groups. From having no apparent existence before 1880, they became politically prominent just seventy years later, with outstanding individuals occupying key national political positions in the first independent national government. Who, then, were the Tsimihety? What did the term denote? In many ways the question of the identity of Tsimihety is the central question of this book. What I shall try to do in the remainder of this chapter is suggest why and how this question came to be one that could be asked. I shall try to reconstruct, in broad terms, the events and conditions prior to the twentieth century that brought the concept of Tsimihety into being and to historical notice.

The term *Tsimihety* means "those who do not cut their hair." This is patently not a realistic description, at least nowadays. The people who described themselves as Tsimihety did cut their hair and the men also shaved their beards. I was told by some Tsimihety people that the name referred to the fact that during the time of the *Marofelana* bandits, active at the end of the nineteenth century and again at various times more recently, men let their hair grow long so that in the dark they might be mistaken for women and so not be attacked. One problem with this explanation is that Tsimihety women in 1963 wore their hair in a traditional style said to always have been in vogue, and this style was combed and plaited up on the head. During the Marofelana, however, women as well as men could have worn their hair hanging down. Another explanation, found in the literature as well as repeated to me orally, is that unlike other Malagasy, particularly Sakalava, Tsimihety did not shave their hair as a sign of mourning on the death of a *mpanjaka* or monarch. To not cut one's hair on such an occasion was also to proclaim one had no loyalty or allegiance to the monarch or to his or her successor. Generalized this would mean that "Tsimihety" applied to people who, in contrast to most other Malagasy and certainly in contrast to neighboring Sakalava and Betsimisaraka, had some sort of egalitarian political life, or even an apolitical life.

At least one writer, Raymond Kent, accepts this general form of explanation and tries to specify the time and place of its emergence. It was the refusal of some people to acknowledge the rule of the Maroserana, founders of the numerous kingdoms in the west of Madagascar, that led to these recalcitrants being termed "Tsimihety" (Kent 1970:190–91). I doubt the correctness of this suggestion, however, because Maroserana were prominent in the 1600s, and there is no mention (that I can find) of Tsimihety before the late 1800s. What is more, the Maroserana founded dynasties in the *west* of Madagascar, whereas all the documentary, genealogical, and oral evidence that I could gather indicates an *eastern* origin for Tsimihety (cf. Feeley-Harnik 1982:32). However, I think Kent's general hypothesis that Tsimihety indicates a refusal to acknowledge hierarchical authority is plausible. But, if the circumstances did not occur in the sixteenth century and did not originate on the west coast, what are the more likely possibilities?

The London Missionary Society Station, which was the headquarters and base of Donald Schofield's work, was situated a few kilometers outside Mandritsara. Mandritsara was the district capital and was also the chief settlement of the acknowledged heartland of Tsimihety, Androna. Although many Malagasy other than Tsimihety lived in Mandritsara and Androna—Merina, Betsileo, Betsimisaraka, Sihanaka, Antandroy, Makoa—Tsimihety of Androna considered themselves authentic Tsimihety, *Tsimihety ny Tsimihety,* and were so regarded by others living elsewhere. All my information comes from Androna and, even if it should prove to be inaccurate from another point of view, it reflects what authentic Tsimihety considered to be the case.

Thus without exception the place of origin of Tsimihety in Androna was agreed as being Ivongo, an area on the east coast that included

Mananara, Maroantsetra, and Nosi Mangabe. The first are small towns, and the last is a small island. The vast majority of Tsimihety genealogies referred back to ancestors originating from this area, and many Tsimihety *foko* claimed to have tombs in this area on the east coast, even though few admitted these tombs were still active and used by them for burials.

A composite of my fieldnotes containing accounts by old men of the origin of the Tsimihety is as follows:

> A ship was wrecked at Foulepointe (south of Mananara) and the survivors came ashore. They were not well received by the local Betsimisaraka, however. These white sailors fled north to Ivongo where they married Antemananara and Antevongo girls. This gave rise to the *foko* Karanimalandy. The sailors, their wives and descendants lived peaceful and settled lives and were led by a *sojabe* or chief. Some time later, because of many quarrels with other villages and other chiefs, some of the Karanimalandy left their villages. Many more started to leave when the Merina came. Some of those who fled went north to Ambodihazomamy, while others, led by Ramarohosina came west, through the forest and settled in Vohilava (the eastern edge of Androna).

This general account agrees with that recorded by Magnés in the same region (1953) and repeated by Grandidier (1958). But there is one significant difference. Magnés suggests that it was Sihanaka people who fled north to Ivongo and thence came to Androna, not Betsimisaraka and Europeans. This would imply a place of origin to the south, not the east, and so would conflict with a Tsimihety outlook to the east. In circumstantial support of the part European and eastern origin of Tsimihety is the recorded arrival, in 1774, in the Baie d'Antongil (i.e., the east coast) of a Polish-Hungarian adventurer, Baron de Benyowski, and his crews. Benyowski and some of his men settled near Maroantsetra, where they were said to have built their own village, which they called Louisbourg. Presumably they took local girls.

Benyowski himself, who had previously marauded in Manchuria, offered to conquer the whole island for France and, from time to time, sent progress reports of his conquests to Paris, even though he never moved out of Louisbourg. Benyowski himself did not last long in Madagascar, but it is quite possible some of his men stayed, and even more probable that they fathered children.

By 1800 the northeast coast of Madagascar was not only the outlet to the rest of the world for the Merina interior, it was also the scene of political and economic competition between Britain and France, was the entrepôt for the slave trade, and was an area of volatile local activity. In 1814, the British attempted to establish a settlement and in 1817 an accord was reached between the British and the Merina King Radama I. By this accord the slave trade was to end and Radama I was guaranteed recognition as the ruler of the whole of Madagascar. Given these maneuverings, trading, and rivalries, the northeast coast of Madagascar was probably a difficult place for locals to live in, and it is not too unlikely that some would have left the area.

My notes of conversations with Tsimihety and references to written sources suggest the following course of events to the west.

In the late 1700s and early 1800s the Sakalava of the west coast were undergoing a time of great turmoil and unrest. The Zafinimena of Boeni had been driving the Zafinifotsy of Menabe slowly north for many years. Eventually the retreating Zafinifotsy came more or less to a full stop at the banks of the Sofia River. On the eastern side of the river were the Vohilava, led by Ramarohosina. The Zafinifotsy asked for, and were given permission to settle across the Sofia, and the alliance was cemented by the marriage of Ramarohosina to the Zafinifotsy princess Tompo or Renimanana.

However while the marriage was being celebrated in Antsirabe in Vohilava, the Zafinimena attacked Renimanana's brothers at Mahajamba and defeated them. As a result of this defeat the Zafinifotsy were put in disarray: one group under Ramaitso fled to Maringibato, on the western fringe of Androna, another group under Ralambo went to Befandriana and a fourth group pushed north to the Antankarana. But though the Zafinifotsy were routed, Renimanana and her Vohilava husband, Ramarahosina, and their followers (both Zafinifotsy and Vohilava) were still a force to be reckoned with. When the Zafinimena moved across the river they were defeated by the alliance whose victory created an even greater solidarity between them. Their unity was signified by their single name, Antandrona, and the area in which they claimed to rule was known as Androna.

Grandidier gives a similar account, which he bases on Magnés (1953). Magnés's account is based largely on oral accounts and could well include some from the same people I spoke with. Grandidier makes one further statement—that the Zafinifotsy would be granted asylum so long as they laid no claim to land. If there was any single traditional event common to Tsimihety theorizing about who the Tsimihety were and their origins, it was the marriage between Ramarahosina and Renimanana, which was a union, under crisis circumstances, of two *mpanjaka* or aristocrats, one indigenous and the other from the highest ranking of Sakalava dynasties. Sakalava were considered by Tsimihety to have authentic, hereditary, and divine dynasties. In the light of present Tsimihety political and social egalitarianism, this awe of Sakalava mpanjaka is important for the following question: How and why did Tsimihety come to reject not only kingship and chiefs but every semblance of political hierarchy? Note also that at this time, about 1800, the term used to identify people of the region was originally *Vohilava,* and became *Antandrona.*

Grandidier says that the Antandrona dynasty was not a strong one and had no overall control over people of the region. Instead, he suggests, there were numerous independent groups loosely linked together and there were chiefs rather than kings. This is certainly a pattern similar to that of the Betsimisaraka who recognized only local chiefs in 1963 and probably did so in the past. But, unless the Zafinifotsy agreed to dilute their ideas of monarchy and aristocracy as part of their acceptance by the Vohilava, as well as forgo claims to land, it is strange that such a strongly ritualized and hereditary institution as the Sakalava dynasty and its mpanjakas should fade so quickly.

In 1820 another treaty was signed between Radama I and the British. The British agreed to help Radama professionalize his army and to supply military equipment. This meant he was able to begin his successful subjugation of the Sakalava of the west, the Bezanozano and Sihanaka of the northeast, and the Betsimisaraka of the east coast. He invaded the Betsimisaraka in 1823. While Radama was advancing on all sides against other Malagasy people, the French, in opposition to the British, had stepped up their efforts to establish both commercial and political interests in Madagascar. They established a settlement on the Isle St. Marie, in the Baie d'Antongil, which was also an attempt on their part to put a stop to Betsimisaraka piracy (Deschamps 1961:156).

Estimating twenty years per generation, many Tsimihety genealogies suggested an intensifying emigration from Mananara and Maroantsetra from 1820 on, that is during these disturbances of the northeast areas of Mananara and Maroantsetra or Ivongo.

In 1824 Radama turned his attention to Androna, which he occupied without meeting any resistance. The popular account of the origin of the name *Mandritsara* attributes it to this nonresistance. "Mandritsara ato" is "the place were one sleeps well," i.e., without any fear of attack. By all accounts the people living in Androna accepted the Merina presence and agreed to pay a small tax (*vary zehy*) and to provision Merina troops and the garrison that Radama installed at Marotandrano, the place which commanded the route south through the forest. Grandidier thinks that the reason there was no resistance on the part of the people of Androna was because they were involved in petty disputes and welcomed the pacifying presence of the Merina. This is plausible but unsupported.

Few of the people I spoke to knew the name Radama, but many mentioned the *komandy* of the garrison at Marotandrano. He was cited to me for his cruelty and his actions were given as one of the reasons why the Merina became so disliked. The story of his practice of summoning people before him, making them crawl up to him, and then springing them into a trap so that they fell down onto a bed of spikes was told me countless times.

It is likely that some Merina were oppressive toward the people of Androna and that this story is illustrative of the sort of behavior which explains the *volteface* from welcoming the Merina to detesting them. This change is fundamental to understanding the emergence of Tsimihety as a people and as a concept.

Grandidier writes that soon after the Merina arrival there were numerous, scattered rebellions by Antandrona against Merina. All of these were savagely repressed. So humiliating was the way in which the Merina put down any opposition that there was a rash of suicides by Antandrona/Vohilava chiefs (Grandidier 1958:128, n.l). Grandidier does not use a Malagasy term and so these "chiefs" cannot be identified as either mpanjaka or *soja,* a point of some importance. It is taken for granted, though, that Antandrona groups were led by individuals with authority, that there was some sort of hierarchical political organization at this time. I find from my notes that some men spoke of mpanjaka leading *foko* against the Merina, and that in some cases where I pressed the point they were specified as relatives of Ramarohosina. This would hint that these were people living in the west of Androna who had incorporated Zafinifotsy into their lineage.

Following the wholesale decapitation of Antandrona groups, the

Merina established their own appointees as "chiefs" or *komandy,* their lieutenants (*lefitra komandy*), *komandy borizano,* and finally each village was placed under the supervision of the indigenous elders (*andriambaventy*) (Grandidier 1958:128, n.1). As might have been expected there were disputes between komandy that led to the setting up of military posts whose troops could operate against any neighboring disputants, but these probably did not involve Antandrona. However, by this time (1830 onward?) Androna had become an unstable area in which raids, fighting, and violence were more or less the order of the day. According to my oral historians, the Merina took it out on the Antandrona and were often very cruel. The cruelty of the Merina is the constantly recurring theme of any discussion of the history among present-day Tsimihety. People offered no specific information about events or persons between the period of the establishment of Merina rule and the coming of the French in 1895-96.

At that time the Merina Governor Rakotovoalavo sought the cooperation of Antandrona/Vohilava against the French, but they refused. Accordingly Rakotovoalava threatened the execute the "chef" Bosy Iadanitsimiady, who promptly fled to Majunga. Grandidier says the French under Pradon advanced into Androna from Maroantsetra, reaching Mandritsara on December 18, 1896, where Bosy was freed (Grandidier 1958:129). My notes give a different story. People rallied under the *sojabe* (i.e., chief) Manampiro and threatened to assist the French if Rakotovoalavo did not withdraw his threat against mpanjaka Bosy. Rakotovoalavo agreed and the Antandrona did not help the French. However, upon his return from Majunga Bosy welcomed the French in Mandritsara. Meanwhile another *soja,* Radoany of Befandriana, did fight with the French against the Merina.

By the late 1890s the people of Antandrona still retained a deep-seated hatred of the Merina, which suggests the Merina had managed to maintain a steady, if volatile, rule over the region. A second factor of importance in the light of contemporary matters is that there seemed to have been two parallel forms of political hierarchy: the Merina administration, including the army and its commanders, and the indigenous "chiefs" that may have included mpanjakas and *sojas,* though it is possible that the indigenous hierarchy may have had to operate in a somewhat covert fashion because of its inherent threat to the Merina authority.

No sooner had the French been welcomed to Androna and Mandritsara than there were outbreaks of protest and rebellion against them, though exactly which groups rebelled is not clear. I have several differing accounts of Pradon's policy. The first account suggests that Pradon, recognizing the firm establishment of Sakalava mpanjakas as rulers with deep, traditionally respected authority, appointed Sakalava mpanjakas as his local indigenous officials in Mandritsara. This made some sense from his point of view as the French set up their provincial capital in Ivongo. However, according to some of my respondents, the Sakalava were implacably opposed to rule by outsiders such as the French, and the mpanjakas plotted to kill all Europeans. They were found out, tried, and executed. But other people told me that Pradon and the Sakalava got along very well together. As well, Pradon appointed a special Merina official in 1897 to manage commercial affairs in the region since most local commerce was carried out by Merina.

Grandidier's account supports the first of my accounts. In 1897 Mandritsara was attacked and its garrison had to be reinforced. The Sakalava mpanjaka Ndrianjalahy rebelled; the French military commander Gouraud was murdered in Bealanana and his headquarters burned down. In retaliation the French put the whole area under military rule, building a number of strategically placed military outposts (1958: 129–30).

Although the conditions of their presence are uncertain it is agreed by all sources that Sakalava rulers were brought into Androna, and though they did not come as conquerors, as did the Merina, they were introduced by the French as their agents and as outsiders. One way or another they fomented trouble, and so between 1896 and 1900, Androna's people had been, or were being, dominated by officials of three outside groups— Merina, French, and Sakalava. Their own chiefs had not had a happy time either: a number of them had committed suicide, several had had to flee, and some had been killed. Up until this time the indigenous people of the region had been variously referred to as Vohilava, Antandrona, and Betsimisaraka. With the establishment of French rule reference is made variously to Tsimihety/Betsimisaraka or to Tsimihety in historical works such as those by Grandidier and also in administrative records and oral accounts. There is also the sense that under the French administration the area of Androna (between the Sofia River on the west, the eastern forest, the southern forest at Marotandrano, and the northern escarpment) was being treated as a loose political entity, and this treatment called forth a matching unified response. Smaller groups being treated alike perceived in this treatment a common interest and concern,

a common history. This, too, was reflected in the emergence of a common
name, Tsimihety. The term itself could have gained currency because the
Sakalava mpanjakas put in authority by the French were not accepted
as the dynastic and ritual rulers by the Antandrona. Ritual acceptance
and legitimacy would, among other things, be marked by shaving the
head on the death of the mpanjaka. This departure from Sakalava tradition was a prominent marker of difference and identity between Vohilava
and Sakalava, and a reminder that it was the Sakalava who had sought
asylum from the Vohilava and accepted a subordinate position. By putting
Sakalava mpanjakas in positions of authority over Vohilava the French
were overturning the proper order of history. "Tsimihety" reaffirmed that
proper order.

At the same time as the institution of French authority was an
immediate consequence of French conquest, the disbanding of the Merina
army followed naturally. Many Merina soldiers, instead of returning to
Imerina, took to the bush and lived off not only the countryside but
also off its inhabitants—by robbing, ambush, and violence. These gangs
were known as *Marofelana* and, in 1963, there were still some people
alive who remembered these Marofelana from their childhood. The Marofelana, it was said, attacked mostly at night or at dawn. They would
enter a village, kill any men they found, and steal whatever supplies
they could find. To avoid Marofelana people frequently did not sleep in
the villages but went up into the hills, where they camped overnight in
the caves and on the rock ledges. I was taken to one of these caves
under strict secrecy because they were still in use in 1963 to avoid such
officials as policemen. The one I saw had a floor that was littered with
pottery, much of it half-buried, and it could well have been used many
years ago as a living quarter. However the other ruse used to avoid the
marofelana was said to have been the practice by males of growing their
hair long so as to be mistaken for women in the darkness of the night
or the gloom of dawn; the people Androna thus became known by their
subterfuge of not cutting their hair to avoid being murdered by roving
brigands. Although this is the most "popular" derivation of their name
among Tsimihety with whom I spoke, I doubt that such a strategy would
be unique to the people of Androna, as there were disbanded Merina
soldiers at large all over Madagascar. The ruse itself is unlikely to have
made much difference to identification in the dark, and although the
people did suffer at the hands of the Marofelana, this was not an experience unique to them. Neither was it something of such deep emotional and

political import as the continuing efforts by *vazaha* or outsiders to impose their will and the matching response of resistance by the Antandrona.

The evolution of Tsimihety, the coming into being of both the concept and the social entity it was intended to signify, might be summarized as follows. Before the conquest by the Merina the area of Androna was peopled by small independent groups, of whom the most significant were the Vohilava. After the Merina conquest of the east coast there was an influx of immigrants. At the same time Antandrona/Vohilava joined up with Sakalava (Zafinifotsy) and were accorded a dominant position vis-à-vis the Sakalava Zafinifotsy. Under the Merina a single but external authority was placed over the region, which imposed on it a vague sense of unity but not unification. Unification as a sense of sharing a common experience (of oppression from, and resistance to, outsiders) grew under Merina rule and was reinforced with the coming of the French, whose establishment of Sakalava mpanjaka as local authorities in the area crystallized not only the tradition of a common experience but also the sense of common opposition. The distinction between Vohilava, who did not cut their hair as a sign of ritual recognition of mpanjaka, and the Sakalava, who did, was indicated in Malagasy by the term *tsimihety,* and this became elevated into an "ethnic" name. French, Sakalava, and Merina officials may have used the term to describe "locals," and the locals, in turn, adopted the term to identify themselves.

This designation may have been reinforced by the term's appropriate description of the ruse used by people to fool the Marofelana. Admittedly such a derivation is no more than informed guesswork. But the real point is not whether this is the way Tsimihety came into being or not, but that Tsimihety was a recent term and the people it referred to were not, and did not, necessarily see themselves as a solidary political or ritual group, such as a tribe with special criteria of exclusiveness. This is true in spite of the fact that modern maps may indicate *Tsimihety* and pick out with solid or dotted lines a territorial boundary. The example is certainly not unique. Kottak notes that the Betsileo "tribe" was a product of the Merina expansion (1980:48), and Eggert writes that the so-called Mahafaly were mistakenly named because "the first Europeans to write about the region may have mistaken the word its people used to describe their homeland for a name used to describe themselves as a group" (Eggert 1986:333).

From the time of the establishment of French rule, the sources available for reconstruction of Tsimihety include primary documents written by French officials. With some reservation I was allowed to consult some of the records and annual reports written by the sous-prefet of Mandritsara. I am grateful for this privilege, but I must also add that I was not allowed to see some of the reports and certain other records. There was no reason why I should have been given access, and there may well have been good reasons why I should not.

French colonial policy for Madagascar was formulated by General Gallieni, the first governor. It assumed that all Malagasy people followed the same sociopolitical system, and it tacitly assumed that the Malagasy were like all other colonial people. The basic assumption was that indigenous people recognized some form of hierarchy and that they were divided into territorial groupings. Granted these assumptions, Gallieni's policy was founded on two principles: (1) *politique des races,* which required that, as far as possible, native people should be governed indirectly, through their own institutions and officials. One consequence of this was that all French officials were obliged to make a careful study of the culture and society of the people they were to govern and administer; (2) *tache d'huile,* a policy that, assuming hierarchy, specified that orders should percolate down the ranks and the needs of the governed, seep up the ranks. What, however, if the indigenous people had no traditional hierarchy through which to rule? Colonial management would evaporate into thin air, and people's demands, if they had any, would have nowhere to go.

The sketchy impression I gained from trying to reconstruct the early history of Tsimihety, and which I have tried to convey above, is of an indigenous hierarchy gradually weakening during the course of the nineteenth century. In the east of Androna, where Betsimisaraka immigrants were predominant, chiefship was probably on a narrow, local scale and hierarchy not strongly marked. To the west, where Sakalava influence increased, chiefship and hierarchy were more clearly defined and may even have been comparable to the Sakalava mpanjaka dynasties. But the imposition of Merina komandy and appointees, and later the appointment of Sakalava by the French to political leadership, seems clearly to have brought about some sort of reaction from the people, who were being more and more frequently identified as Tsimihety. They did not recognize the authority of either Merina or French appointees, even though these were Malagasy rather than Europeans; they were still *other* Malagasy. Tsimihety could have covertly stuck to their own chiefs and followed them as leaders of an alternative, but authentic, polity. But this did not happen because, as I said above, Androna hierarchies were in disarray, and it is quite possible that traditional office was not lineage-based and hence not founded on permanent title. With the establishment of French rule it seems that the relatively unsuccessful Androna hierarchical organization faded away, but this did not mean that the administration's appointees, the Sakalava, could just walk in and occupy the traditional position of chief. They were the Malagasy outsiders and the agents of even more foreign outsiders, the French. As if by tacit agreement not only the Androna hierarchy disappeared, but with the resentment against outside appointees stirred up at the same time, the very idea of chiefs, kings, rulers, governors, district officers—the idea of hierarchy itself—was rejected. The Androna/Vohilava became Tsimihety people who, while not necessarily positive about egalitarianism, were people who came to direct their social and political lives on an egalitarian basis, dispensing with the guidance and authority of leaders. With this happening, probably quite unintentionally, the effectiveness of the principles of French government became severely undermined. Instead of a continuous and integrated hierarchy envisaged by Gallieni in which indigenous and French administrators formed a harmonious administration, among the Tsimihety there arose instead a Tsimihety way of life that bypassed a French or vazaha hierarchy, and in the course of this bypass developed itself into an independent society. How this independence emerged, intensified, and supported itself without being hostile and openly rebellious to the French is what I set out to describe and analyze in the following chapters.

French occupation was not a disinterested and high-minded mission to convert others to French culture. It had, like the colonial enterprise in general, materialistic and commercial motives. Soon after the occupation, merchants and company agents were encouraged to come to Mandritsara to set up agencies. In 1912 an agency of the Societé Pastorale was established with the object of buying cattle and, to further this objective, to raise the standard of rearing and the quality of cattle. In the same year a model rice field was started to show Tsimihety how to cultivate rice more efficiently so that they could produce surplus for export. New, higher quality grains were also introduced. Traders were invited to set up shop in Mandritsara to sell imported goods and create the impetus for a cash economy. Entrepreneurs were welcomed; as a result a graphite mine was opened near Marotandrano, and raphia plantations were started with a view to exporting the fiber and oil from the kernel. In 1936 an extensive project involving model nurseries in twenty-three locations throughout Androna was initiated. The aim was to demonstrate to Tsimihety how such cash crops as peanuts, kapok, coffee, vanilla, and good-quality vegetables could be profitably and effectively grown. During all this time concessions were granted to expatriate Frenchmen and Merina, not only so that they could make a good living but so that their example might encourage Tsimihety.

As far as I can tell not one of these projects achieved its intended purpose: to convert Tsimihety to a rationalized mode of production and consumption so that they would become involved in the cash economy, to produce a surplus for export (and to pay a tax), and to learn to want to consume manufactured products from France. Not even ploughs, which were distributed free for use in rice fields, were adopted. Instead, most of them ended up protruding, half-buried, from the ground in Tsimihety villages. Comments on these efforts to improve Tsimihety betray the frustration of administrators: "le repose est son (Tsimihety) occupation favorite," "c'est impossible d'encourager Tsimihety," "le Tsimihety paleolithique."

In 1929 the sous-prefet wrote that the Tsimihety respected authority and were quite obedient; yet later in his report he described Tsimihety as being jealous of their freedom and complained that they consistently refused to work! In 1950 the annual report contained six complaints about the difficulty of collecting taxes because Tsimihety flit into the forest whenever any officials come into view, or even before then, and the indigenous chefs de village could not be trusted to collect any monies. In that same year three "collective rurales" were organized, two in Mandritsara and one in Kalandy. The aim was to galvanize people by organization and example into producing for profit. Within four months all three had collapsed.

These administration-inspired projects failed not because Tsimihety openly resisted them or stayed away but because they stonewalled and blocked. They planted kapok, but harvested only what they thought they needed; they joined the collective but did very little work; they came to see the model rice field but carried on preparing their own fields in their own way; they walked around the nurseries and admired them but made no attempt to copy the techniques of planting. I was both witness and "victim" of this sort of tactic myself—people would agree or promise enthusiastically to do something, or to turn up, but when the time came, they were nowhere to be seen. Whether this attitude and conduct was intentional and cultural, rather than a factor of individual psychology or a Tsimihety trait originating in the development of a strategy of independence, is something to be pondered later.

During the early years of the French occupation, between 1896 and 1912, Androna was governed from Ivongo, on the east coast. All communications and travel were along routes east. This, no doubt, facilitated migration into Androna by Betsimisaraka who "became" Tsimihety. Then, in 1912, the French transferred their administration from east to west, and Majunga became the provincial seat of government. The routes east to Mananara fell into disuse for trade, but people still traveled into Androna from the east. The registers for this time, however, indicated a migration of up to ten thousand people annually *from* Androna westward across the Sofia; yet at the same time the census figures indicate a rapid rise in the population of Androna.

The Tsimihety settlement pattern posed problems for the French from the beginning. The 1911 report described the preference of Tsimihety for living in dispersed households for a short time, their penchant for moving frequently, so much so that the report describes them as *nomadic,* a term also used to describe them in general accounts (cf. Deschamps 1961:292). They were said to be willing to abandon their wooden houses on any pretext, moving with their cattle and a few household belongings. They only seemed to own land temporarily, for as long as they cultivated it, and all this, as was pointed out to superiors in Majunga, made administration very difficult. Virtually the same comments were made in the report of 1927, with the added note that whenever Tsimihety were asked to do something, they readily agreed but then, as soon as the officials left, they would abandon the hamlet! To counteract this tendency of dispersal the French encouraged settlement in larger, more permanent villages, but exactly the same attitudes and tactics were used by Tsimihety during my fieldwork time (1962–63) as had been complained of in 1911 and 1927. This shared "character" of Tsimihety is summed up by Louis Molet, the principal ethnographer of Tsimihety:

> Avec les Tsimihety on ne discute pas; on donne des ordres et les ordres sont exécutés ou ne sont pas. On va voire les gens, ils se sont pas chez eux; on les convoque, ils ne viennent pas. (Molet 1959:155)

There seems to have been relatively little violent opposition on the part of Tsimihety. In 1926 it was reported that numerous Merina living in Androna had had their cattle slaughtered. Then, in 1947, there was the widespread and bloody revolt of the Malagasy against the French. There is no direct acknowledgment of Tsimihety taking part in any violence. But there are, on the other hand, both written and oral accounts of skirmishes between Moroccan and Senegalese troops with rebels in and near the forest at Marotandrano that could have involved Tsimihety. Certainly the cruelty of Senegalese is well remembered by Tsimihety, and the personal name *Senegaly* was frequently given to men born at about this time. What people did remember was the widespread outbreak of *tromba* or trance possession at this time. Tromba were organized into named "cells" of leaders and followers. There are records of what could well have been revenge tactics pursued by Merina against Tsimihety. For example, in 1927 the administration noted that Merina merchants were exploiting Tsimihety, and in 1950 many Merina tried to use the courts to expropriate Tsimihety land.

The Independent Republic of Madagascar was declared on June 16, 1960, and its first president, Philibert Tsiranana, sworn in. President Tsiranana was a Tsimihety born in a village in Androna, and his leadership, put in a national context, represented the success of the periphery and the provinces against the Merina center. That the egalitarian Tsimihety should produce the first national leader was something of an irony, even a contradiction. But it was the lack of enthusiasm for this achievement by Tsimihety that I knew which puzzled me; indeed some men were downright hostile to Tsiranana in private, though never in public. They seemed to think of him as a vazaha, an outsider, though when he came to visit Mandritsara he made great play of being Tsimihety, a country boy like members of his audience.

Trying to Understand Tsimihety

Tsimihety were not the only people in Madagascar to pursue their politics without hierarchy, though in so doing they were in a minority. Their immediate neighbors, the Sakalava, had been adamant in preserving their institutions of hereditary monarchy in spite of all the Merina and French could do to discourage them. The Betsimisaraka, eastern neighbors, observed a political and social organization based on a weak form of chiefship, but they also recognized a stronger form of hierarchy through their recognition of, and obedience to, *tromba* or shamans.

Tsimihety remained uninfluenced yet remarkably adaptable, for when they went to live among the Sakalava they readily observed the authority of the mpanjaka and served in her court. It was clear from the history of Androna that Antandrona and Vohilava, precursors of Tsimihety, recognized a hierarchical organization with chiefs, and possibly mpanjaka, so what had happened in the past hundred years or so was a political devolution from hierarchy to acephalous organization. I have hinted at some of the reasons why this may have occurred, though overall it is more than likely that this devolution was an unintended and unanticipated consequence of other actions and events. This devolution seemed coincidental with the emergence of the concept and the people— Tsimihety—and, more surprisingly, with the almost unbelievable expansion of Tsimihety, both geographically and demographically—from 35,000 to between 400,000 and 700,000 just sixty years later. Classically such populations have been politically organized in segmentary form, an expanding series of nesting groups based on similar criteria of recruitment and membership, notably descent. (The Nuer are the paradigm; see Evans-Pritchard 1940.) A segmentary organization supports an ideology of unity, of the singleness of the entire population as "the people" or, in anthropologist's terms, the "tribe." Tsimihety, in spite of references to them as "un peuple" or their location on a "carte ethnique" circumscribed within the conventional dotted lines, had no idea among themselves that they were a political or a social entity in any sense that could theoretically lead to their mobilization. They did not recognize a segmentary organization of nesting social groups linked together through genealogies, and no anthropologist's segmentary model could fit them together. Tsimihety was not an organization with functions; it had no structure in which its members "did" things and thereby played parts in a whole, in which activity gave them their identity and their place. Rather Tsimihety denoted a *set*. Members of a set are defined solely by virtue of their possessing the particular attributes defining the set (Day 1987:186). As long as the set retains the same attributes its identity remains the same, and individuals who possess these attributes remain members of the set. So, in understanding Tsimihety, it is appropriate to identify attributes rather than to assume and analyze the functions of either individuals or groups. Neither act in relation to a systematic whole. A set, however, is distinctive; it is recognizable by its difference from other sets and from organizations. What may well account for the demographic expansion of Tsimihety is that people of nearby regions, especially the east coast, adopted as their own attributes the attributes that identified Tsimihety. The principal attribute was their denial of the validity to their lives of authority exercised through hierarchy. The immediate and desired consequence of this denial was the achievement of individual and small-group independence and liberty. Denial of authority is not, however, a purely ideological factor. For freedom to be a fact, people have to act pragmatically. Since Tsimihety came into being there is little or no evidence that people opposed authority through violence or through secret rituals that, as it were, created an alternative structure (as is the case among the Betsimisaraka described by Althabe 1969). Either way required an organization that would hinge them too firmly to the outside. Their opposition and their freedom were secured at one and the same time by overt means, but without organization. And yet, there was no evidence that Tsimihety had ever descended into anarchy or had been riddled with internal dissent. Whatever the relation between attributes and actions it has worked as part of real, everyday life and did not exist solely in the realms of theory. Thus, I see as part of my task to reconstruct from my fieldnotes the means by which Tsimihety maintained their independence from outside influence in their everyday lives—how they simultaneously resisted the outside without tangling with it, without organizing, and without providing the French (or the central government) with an opponent. To have done so would have been to have put themselves into a structural, adversarial relationship, and this would have made them not only dependent, but subordinate.

Yet at the same time they followed some sort of "culture," which held their social lives together, ensured a satisfactory distribution of resources, provided individuals with recourse to justice, afforded spiritual sustenance, and which was stamped with a certain style that made it possible for people to identify their sameness as a difference from all others, what Tsimihety call *fomba Tsimihety,* Tsimihety tradition.

CHAPTER 2

Liberté

The central problem in classical political thought is the reconciliation of the individuality and freedom of the human being with the necessity to live socially, with others, in an orderly fashion. Rousseau found his solution in the notion of the general will, which Kant abstracted into the obedience to self-made, universalizable rules. Since the nineteenth century discovery of the descent group (the gens, the clan, the tribe, or the lineage), it has been suggested that in the earlier stages of society the individual has no individuality other than that which is acquired from the group. This position was formalized by Marx and later Marxists. A man or woman without a group is not a person. Such a position is asserted with conviction still—for example, Peter Berger writes of "traditional" society that "an individual human being *is* his collective identification" (1986:92). The classical view posits freedom under law; the second dismisses individual freedom as simply a nonstarter as far as "traditional" society is concerned. Both are, to put it mildly, a little beyond the application and practice of the "ordinary man." Certainly anthropologists studying "traditional" societies have not only met "individuals," they have also run up against the awkward individualism of the people they are living with. The idea of the unfree traditional society has its early modern formulation in the work of Frazer, for whom all societies without modern science were living in a world that they did not understand, hence leaving everything to fate and closing their minds with superstition. Science liberates because it frees people from beliefs in fate, or, as Berger puts it: "one of the most fundamental traits of modernization is a vast movement from fate to choice in human affairs" (Ibid.:86). But, as I have already described, Tsimihety, who fitted the "traditional society" category, were offered Christianity, education for literacy, modern technology, modern methods of horticulture, agriculture and cattle raising, and, for that matter, modern governmental institutions—and, by

33

various ways and means, most people chose to reject them. Their very act of rejection was surely an exercise of their freedom to choose, and neither the Merina nor the French could prevent this freedom, however hard they tried. In spite of oppressive circumstances people were as free to resist outside pressure as they were free to disobey orders. People living in modern, fast-changing societies have tended to think of people without a written history as people without a history at all who have been transfixed in their present mode since Eden. Such a supposed stasis cannot be taken other than as evidence for a lack of freedom, a servitude to custom and tradition. Archaeology is, however, a record of change among preliterate, prehistorical societies and of their forms of freedom. This may take one of two forms: resistance to outside incursion, which represents the choice to retain present ways, or adaptation to changes, which must involve the recognition of options and the exercise of choice. A third possibility is, of course, a mixture of the two. Human adaptation must be the exercise of choice, the freedom to make a mistake. In the Malagasy situation, for example, individual Malagasy chose to adapt to French rule in different ways: by assimilating to it, by opposing it, by appearing to go along with it while developing underground forms of opposition or alternatives. Tsimihety chose a distinctive way of adjusting to and manipulating the political context that was constantly changing around them, partly by their own actions, partly by virtue of events beyond their influence.

Freedom begins with human relations, with the relation between any individual and the context of other people with whom he or she comes into some sort of contact. Thus, to consider basic freedom among Tsimihety one must accept their dependency on land and then look to see in what ways the organization of relations between people impeded or opened the access of individuals to land; then, in what way the presence of outsiders affected relations between people with respect to land; and then in what way Tsimihety relations to land were adjusted (or did not need adjusting) to take account of the presence and possible threat of outsiders.

The Countryside

The gathering together of people now known as Tsimihety in the region of Androna was largely the result of immigration of Sakalava from the west, Betsimisaraka from the east, and, in far less significant numbers, Sihanaka and Merina from the south. These immigrants originally joined people already living sparsely in Androna, who were known as Anti- vohilava. Records, demography, and oral accounts also indicate a continuing emigration westward into Sakalava country of people from Androna. This suggests that there were few, if any, ecological, economic, or political constraints on the movement of people throughout a broad stretch of land running across the north central part of Madagascar. Migration north from this area was hampered by a steep escarpment, the Massif de Tsaratanana. To the south there was a band of forest but this did not interfere with Sihanaka coming north, so I conclude Tsi- mihety did not move south because there was no room for them. Political and sentimental ties of Tsimihety to land did not seem to be sufficiently binding as to prevent emigration, or so exclusive as to prevent immi- gration, and outside influences seem to have had neither the will, nor the intention, to inhibit movement. The openness of this territorial band can be contrasted with its overall isolation from the rest of Madagascar, particularly for modern, European-style transport. Much of the eastern forest still remained unmapped, and while the straight line distance between Mandritsara and Mananara on the east coast was 210 kilometers, the traveling distance via vehicular road was 1,452 kilometers. Corre- sponding distances to Maroantsetra were 200 kilometers versus 1,656 kilometers. Bringing in troops or developing a modern transport system for trade, both of which service "development," was severely limited by the nature of the countryside. This explains, in part, the relative extent of the degrees of freedom enjoyed by Tsimihety in coping with the changing influences of the external political context (first Merina, then French, and, finally, the central national government).

At first glance, and in general terms, mobility was more or less uninhibited, and this bespoke of extensive freedom in relation to land. Tsimihety were frequently referred to as nomadic or seminomadic; this was not strictly accurate, however, since they were economically depen- dent on agriculture even though they kept extensive herds of cattle. Cattle, though, were of little importance for subsistence, i.e., meat was not often eaten. In some areas, around the long-established village of Antsirabe on the eastern edge of Androna, a form of slash-and-burn agriculture was practiced, but this did not result in population shifts. Rather, different segments of land within a radius were burned annually so that there was always a permanent population in Antsirabe. Tsimihety nomadism was not comparable to the periodic mobility of slash-and-burn agriculturalists, in which entire communities shift.

Androna was not isolated to those who moved in, out, and around on foot and whose baggage was limited accordingly. People and their cattle moved in and out to live, and those such as Cormorian traders or forest dwellers who brought in salt (made from the rendering of a tree bark to ash), tobacco, and honey to exchange for rice, who limited their stock to what they could carry, found no impediment to mobility. Officials of the bureaucracy, shopkeepers, and entrepreneurs whose stock, manpower, and commissariat requirements were greater than could be transported on foot (except in emergencies) found Androna inaccessible other than by air, so Tsimihety were relatively isolated from them. Almost paradoxically, although the countryside was open to everyone, its topography helped to divide it into naturally separate parts. Much of Androna was split up by small ranges of hills between which were narrow valleys. Each valley was cut off from direct view and contact with its neighbor. The valleys were well watered, and the hills provided grassy slopes for pastures and some, secondary, woodland. People living in a valley have a sense of their privacy and independence from their neighbors as well as from the local center of government and trade, Mandritsara. Although it was not difficult to walk from one valley to the next, it was not a convenient everyday thing to do either because it could often involve a roundabout journey along narrow footpaths. However, a general access through Androna was available along the dirt road that ran roughly east to west from Mandritsara to the Sofia River. The region was also traversed by the Mangarahara River, a tributary of the Sofia with a number of smaller rivers watering the area. Rainfall averaged from about 400 millimeters in January, the height of the wet season, to less than 20 millimeters in June, and temperatures were between 19°C and 26°C, very pleasant and without too great a variation. As a result, the entire region was kept reasonably green.

The very nature of the countryside itself was conducive to instilling a feeling of small-scale separateness, independence, and political privacy. People in a given valley were free to get on with their business without feeling they were under surveillance too often from visitors or neighbors (i.e., other Tsimihety) or officials. And equally it was easy for people to mind their own business. On the other hand, with a slight effort it was easy to visit and move around, while permanent moves had no

insurmountable natural barriers. But if people cultivated land, did not
the investment of their labor make the land their "property" in some
sense? If they dwelt in villages containing substantial houses, did not
this anchor them in some sense? And if valleys had superimposed on
them a pattern of tenure of some sort so as to distribute access and
protect rights, did this not also bring in its wake a form of exclusion
or privilege? These questions relate to the Tsimihety transformation of
the natural landscape into the cultural landscape, and the relation of
this transformation to the conditions of freedom.

The Cultural Landscape

The traditional area of Androna corresponded roughly with the modern
administrative prefecture of Mandritsara, which was made up of five
cantons. My research was carried out in villages in four of these cantons:
Kalandy, Antsirabe, Mandritsara, and Marotandrano. I visited only one
or two villages in the canton of Andohajango. The official area of the
prefecture was 19,400 square kilometers, roughly the size of Androna.
In 1911 the official population was 25,554, of whom 18,231 were designated Tsimihety. The remainder comprised other "ethnic" groups
including: Merina (2,888), Makoa (1,745), and Betsimisaraka (1,690).
By 1950 the population had more than doubled—Tsimihety (47,191),
Merina (2,559), Makoa (5,400), and Betsimisaraka (3,871): total, 63,191.
Such figures, in spite of their apparent precision, are less than reliable
since Tsimihety avoided officials whenever they could, were often on the
move, and tended not to give anything like accurate answers to quantitative questions. In some cases village heads would have provided the
figures, but these were likely to be even less reliable. The vagueness of
these figures can be appreciated from some of the internal contra-
dictions in the actual administrative reports themselves. In 1923 there
were reported to be fifty villages in the canton of Mandritsara with a
total population of 7,658, an average of 153 (which compared to an
average of 106 for Androna). In 1933, Mandritsara had 30 villages with
a population of 11,196 and an average of 376 (compared to an average
for Androna of 286). These figures were intended to show the success
of the policy of gathering people together in larger villages for ease of
administration. In 1911 it was reported that Tsimihety lived in small
hamlets with no more than four or five houses, which they abandoned
on the slightest pretext. In 1927, in between the years during which the

policy of centralization was being pursued, the official report observed that Tsimihety actually lived in even *smaller* hamlets of two or three houses, which made government very difficult. Again it was observed they moved for no apparent reason and so often that they could be described as nomadic. This was, in part, an excuse for why the tax return was so poor.

In 1962–63 we visited 114 villages, mostly in the cantons of Kalandy and Mandritsara. The largest of these was Ankiabe Salohy where we spent several weeks, far more than a census taker would have spent. My estimate of the population was 250. I made no attempt to be seen counting heads anywhere else, but by surreptitious counting I reckoned the average size of a village to be 40. This impression does not agree too closely with the figures given by Molet, who recorded 202 villages in Mandritsara, of which 175 have populations of more than 100 (Molet 1959:83). Molet gives a population density of 5.53 per square kilometer, and though this can be no more than an informed guess that probably errs on the generous side, it gives the right impression, which is that Androna is not densely populated. This is in spite of the widespread claim that Tsimihety are the fastest growing population in the nation (cf. Deschamps 1961:292).

The natural lie of the land was, as I already suggested, a patchwork of valleys and small ranges of hills. The social geography divides this up more geometrically, but less visibly. The central government (*fanja-kana*) divided the land up into provinces, prefectures, subprefectures, districts, cantons, quartiers, and villages, with each of the spatial divisions having its bureaucratic counterpart. Tsimihety superimpose a political geography based on the notion *faritany*. Faritany literally means a boundary or landmark, and it indicated the extent of an area that people claimed for the right to traditional *use*. I emphasize use because they did not claim ownership as a right of disposal, nor did they claim exclusive rights of usage. Faritany were not nested units that could be merged to form larger geopolitical entities; Androna did not consist of amalgamated faritany. Nor were faritany made up of smaller landholding units. The actual boundaries were vaguely defined—usually according to such landmarks as streams, hills, trees, rock outcrops, and the like. But faritany had an identity; they were named, usually after a distinctive landmark, after the principal or original settlement, or sometimes after the first person to establish the faritany. The conditions of such establishment were, most commonly, an arrangement between the settlers and

the presiding mpanjaka or soja and/or immediate neighbors. The existential relevance of the faritany may be gauged from the fact that one
usually cited the name of the faritany in answer to the question: "Where
are you from?" But in answer to the question: "Who are you?" one
cited the name of one's *tanindrazana*.

Tanindrazana also denoted a specific area of land, but rather than
being defined by boundaries it was the range, or circumference of influence, of the ancestors exercised from a centerpoint, the ancestral tomb.
Tanindrazana was not necessarily co-terminous with faritany, which may
include more than one tanindrazana (hence more than one tomb). The
tomb was not literally at the center, just as the boundaries were not
circular, but the ancestors buried in the tomb were the preceding generations who had first settled and then maintained the use of the land.
And the tomb itself was the place where living descendants could expect
to be buried and become ancestors in their turn.

Thus those who could use the land because they would be buried
in its tomb together with those who had used the land were *zafintany,*
the descendants of the land. They were the legitimate and authentic
tenants as distinct from those identified with a different tanindrazana
(*vahiny*) and, especially, from those who were foreign strangers (vazaha
such as Merina and Europeans).

Unlike some other Malagasy people such as Merina, Tsimihety individuals could often lay claim to title in a string of tanindrazana, which,
in effect, marked out the migration routes and settlement points of the
past. I met many people who were zafintany in many places in Androna
as well as back in Mananara, although the claims to tanindrazana in
Mananara were rather more theoretical than real. The multiple membership of Tsimihety in tanindrazana differed from the single entitlement
of the Merina because among the latter the individual had to make a
considerable economic investment in a particular tomb, tombs being
large, elaborate, and expensive. A Merina individual becomes a member
of a single tomb group, and this more or less precludes membership in
other groups (Bloch 1971). In contrast the tomb (*fasana*) among Tsimihety was usually a natural cave or rock shelter in the hills, which was
left virtually unmodified. No investment was required beyond the labor
to make a door and keep it tidy and, in some cases, to construct rough
shelves on which to arrange the coffins. But the tomb for the restless
Tsimihety was the still point of their seminomadic world. Even if they
did not live in the tanindrazana, Tsimihety individuals were sustained

by the knowledge that they belonged to the tanindrazana and the tomb, which was its center. It was there the person knew he or she would be buried and would join the life of the ancestors. To have a right to a tomb and to be able to state just where that is was an important part of the difference between Tsimihety and the other Malagasy who reside in Androna.

The social and political identity that people took as a result of their title to burial in a tomb and right to dwell in a tanindrazana was *zafintany.* This means literally "grandchildren, or descendants, of the land," and its very compounding illustrates its meaning as a territorial and descent identity, with a ritual focus on the tomb. Zafintany were those people, wherever they may actually live, who claimed proprietorship of a particular tanindrazana and the tomb(s) by which it was defined. In any particular case the term would be used spontaneously to differ-entiate the people living in a given place: some were zafintany who were, in a sense, living "at home" in the tanindrazana, and others were vahiny, living as guests. Those who were guests were usually zafintany somewhere else and would, for example, expect to be buried in the tomb of their distant tanindrazana. Conversely, not all who were entitled to the status zafintany were living at home; they may be living as guests elsewhere. In theory zafintany had discretionary rights vis-à-vis vahiny or guests, the latter having to ask permission annually to settle. Zafintany was a status enjoyed by an individual by virtue of ancestral affiliations—a person was zafintany wherever he or she had the father buried, for that was where he or she could claim a right to be buried. Generalized, this extended to an expectation of being buried in the tomb of one's ancestors. This right of burial was extended to the right to live on and cultivate land because it was the land that was opened up and used by the ances-tors. It was important that some zafintany remain in the tanindrazana to continue to keep the land in use. Thus, although the landscape was divided up by boundaries into faritany, and into tanindrazana, there was no sense in which these boundaries confined and hence defined territorial groups of people.

It will be helpful to illustrate with a specific example. Much of my research was carried on in the faritany of Andilamena (see map 2). This faritany included the tanindrazana of the Zafimita (named entities or *foko* will be discussed below) whose fasana was situated in the hills above the valley. The Zafimita, who were zafintany, came originally from the forests around Marotandrano in the south and long before the French.

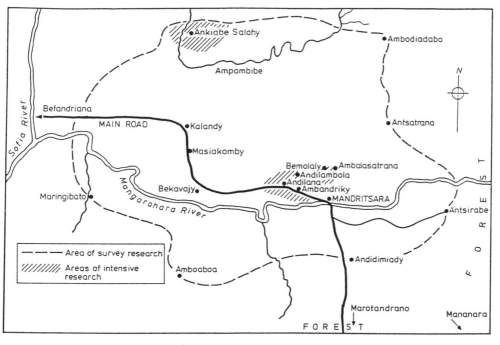

Map 2. Tsimihety research areas

My informant, my adoptive "grandfather" Velo, thought they were of Sihanaka origin and had been driven north by expanding Merina. Arriving in Andilamena, near Mandritsara, they built the village of Andilana and established their tomb in the hills. An approximate reckoning, which I made from Velo's genealogy, was that this took place around 1840. When they arrived the Zafimita sought, and were given, permission to settle by the mpanjaka of Antsirabe, who were Vohilava. Soon after Andilana was founded, new Zafimita immigrants arrived and built a new village nearby, the village of Andampihely. Both villages used the same tomb, and having received the go-ahead from the Vohilava to establish their tomb, the Zafimita became zafintany.

Sometime in the mid-1930s some Zafimita from Andilana left because of a quarrel and went in search of better pastures. They settled in Ambodisobora, about 60 kilometers northwest of Andilana. Here they cleared the land, built a village, and, as far I could gather, sought and received permission from Zafimita in Andilamena to build their own tomb around 1955. Until then they had returned their dead for burial at Andilamena. No mention was made at any time of any contact with Marotandrano, and I never heard of anyone going back there. Velo laughed when I asked whether Zafimita of Andilamena would still consider themselves zafintany at Marotandrano, so for all intents and purposes Zafimita "belong" to Andilamena, but with the commissioning of a tomb at Ambodisobora they became split, zafintany with tanindrazana in two distinct regions. There was still a fairly regular contact between people in Andilamena and Ambodisobora, but this was clearly because there were still close and active kinship ties (Velo had two grandchildren in Ambodisobora), and I suspect the connection would attenuate as the kinship ties became more distant. A third split of the Zafimita occurred when some people from both Andilamena and Andampihely moved off and settled about 35 kilometers southwest, where they built a village called Ambodisohely. The land was thick bush and unclaimed, so they did not ask permission of anyone to settle. They considered that their efforts in clearing the land gave them the right to lay claim to an area they could define as faritany, but they still used the tomb at Andilamena to bury their dead and so did not consider themselves to be zafintany with a tanindrazana. Velo thought it would not be long before they asked permission to build their own tomb, and he would advise his fellow elders to approve when the request came.

Tanindrazana was a plural concept. The same people could speak of their tanindrazana in different parts of Androna, i.e., they were quite different and separate areas of land. But zafintany was a particular form of the unitary concept *foko:* the people of one entity may be divided and resident in different parts of the country such that if they were living on tanindrazana, they were also zafintany. There was only one foko called Zafimita, but they were zafintany in two distinct regions, potential zafintany in a third, and an unknown number lived as vahiny throughout Androna. All who were Zafimita have the same foci—their tomb(s) or fasana in the tanindrazana. At this general level, the possible political function of these concepts was less to foster unity and solidarity and more to facilitate a safe mobility. Thus individuals were free to leave their present homes and fields to settle wherever they wished, but they did not have to sever emotional or spiritual ties to do so: they could always return to their original status and, most importantly, they did not forfeit rights to a final resting place. The dispersion of the foko can be imagined as a drawing out of the lines of migration, people knowing they will be welcome in places where members of the same foko live, and knowing they will enjoy preferred status should their foko be zafin-tany. Migration and mobility among Tsimihety were certainly not random or a leap into the unknown. It was movement along "safe" routes. As I shall discuss later, mobility in 1963 was not one of necessity, determined by outside pressures such as coercion or land shortage. It was a preferred way of life and, because of this, the "structure" of faritany/tanindra-zana/zafintany/foko seemed to function so as to facilitate migration and dispersal rather than to engineer political and social unity. Although many Tsimihety went off and homesteaded rather than move to another established village, they did not isolate themselves spiritually from the place where they were zafintany, since they would expect to be buried in the tomb there and all invocations and remembrances would be directed to the ancestors in the tomb. New tombs were not commissioned unless and until new land and settlements had become well established and their pioneer populations had been resident for at least three gen-erations. (I never came across a case where permission for a new tomb was granted after less than three generations.)

There was some resistance to granting emigrants permission to found their own tombs. Maromaha of Ambodisobora told me that he had been turned down twice by Velo at Andilamena, who gave as the reason that the ancestors in the tomb would be displeased. I came across other instances of such difficulty, and of accompanying frustration. Sometimes the distance between people and their tomb became very inconvenient and frustrating; sometimes people felt it imperative that their "title" be authenticated as zafintany. I found it almost impossible to get reasons why requests should be turned down. In one case the segment of the zafintany who guarded the tomb and the tanindrazana, the segment known as *mpiambinjana* (guardians), to whom the request was made, were very few in number and were trying to encourage some migrants to return.

The place of origin of most Tsimihety is the east coast, particularly Mananara and Maroantsetra. With one or two exceptions of people recently (in the past thirty years) arrived from there, the east was not an active presence. People mentioned Mananara or Maroantsetra in much the same way that New Englanders cite their British ancestry or New Zealanders of Otago cite their Scottish origins. The Vohilava were, how-ever, frequently remembered and cited as the people to whom one owed one's place in Androna. Ramarohosina's tomb at Mahalaina, near Antsir-abe, was looked upon with some awe and reverence. But he was in no way thought of as a founding ancestor or even as a hero to whom Tsimihety owed their deliverance and who, in some way, provided a focus for a singular political identity.

The factual reality of the cultural marking out of the landscape, of the location of distinguishing markers, and of the specification of the situation of people to each other vis-à-vis the land, was one that emphasized fragmentation, dispersal, and migration. The unity came from the common way in which this was done, the recognition that fragmenting, dispersing, and migrating according to organizing concepts such as faritany/tanindrazana/zafintany/foko and fasana was fomba Tsimihety, the Tsimihety tradition. The reference points for superimposing Tsimihety unity will be discussed in chapter 4.

If it was the custom for Tsimihety to move around, and if conceptually coherent entities were in fact scattered, as were the foko, then one would expect close neighbors to be varied in foko terms. This was so. Andilamena can again be the example. Numerically it was dominated by Zafimita, who were zafintany. But they shared this zafintany status with another, smaller, foko—Antanandry, who occupied a small area of the faritany in the east and who had a tomb in the hills. Antanandry were present in much greater strength and with much more land to the north, at Ambalasatrana. Also in Andilamena were vahiny, which included Zafindrabehavana and Zafindramaharatsy, a village of Hova mainty (former lower caste "slaves" of the Merina), and a small village of Makoa. All these were vahiny who had been granted permission by Zafimita to cultivate rice land, to use pastures, and to build their villages. In the case of the Hova mainty and the Makoa it was highly unlikely that Tsimihety would ever request the land back, since both Hova and Makoa villages had been established for over fifty years. In fact the Makoa had their own tomb in the hills. In the case of vahiny Tsimihety, actual permission was not sought every year, but it was implicit in the recognition that they were guests and their status was less than that of the Zafimita. So, just as Androna as a whole was fragmented and there were no structural criteria for conceptualizing it as a political entity, so each village and each faritany was in fact made up of a composite population comprising zafintany and vahiny. There were boundaries, but these staked out zones of influence and served to guide people in rather than to fence them out.

Androna specifically, Tsimihety more generally, was a region that was not a "tribal" or "national" territory but a sphere of influence.

That influence is fomba Tsimihety, Tsimihety culture. Associated with this region, and especially enshrined in the tombs, were the similar, often shared, histories of individual achievement, pride, failure, and humiliation that made up the lives of the ancestors. It was not, however, a collective pride. There was no record in myth or history of Tsimihety ever combining against intruders or building a tradition. Tsimihety were people, individuals, who had pursued similar solutions to similar problems and who had, therefore, developed a sympathy that was backed by crisscrossing kinship ties and drawn-out descent connections. This sympathy made them more willing to cooperate with one another, without feeling obliged to do so, and more particularly, this sympathy gave individuals the confidence to resist attempts by outsiders to govern them. It did not give them a desire to observe a common government, but it circulated among them a common intuition that the preservation of their individual freedom from external dictates and authority was best attained by following certain practices. Collectively these practices were legitimated as fomba Tsimihety. Basic among these was the management of land, the primary resource. How was land managed so as to maintain both individual liberty and subsistence? How was it managed so as to keep to a minimum disputes, which called for the exercise of power and left a way open for outside intervention? How was it managed so as to be equably distributed and protected without becoming exclusive property, and hence the basis for exploitative power?

Freedom and Equity

It is often argued that equality is a straitjacket on freedom, that, for example, it imposes sameness and therefore "limits the boundless variety of human nature" (Hayek 1960/1976:86). But differences incompatible with equality depend entirely on subjective claims and an audience's appraisal. If differences are regarded as incommensurable they cannot be made a basis for inequality. Or, if property is not understood as wealth, all the property in the world does not make one person wealthier than, or superior to, any other. A similar objection to equality is made by Nozick when he claims that insisting on equal access to, and distribution of, material resources limits the freedom of people to use their initiative and imagination, or their right to secure their well-being in a way that is up to them (Nozick 1974). If novel ways of securing well-being are looked on with indifference by traditionalists (instead of, say, being envied or emulated), unequal access to resources makes no difference, so long as the traditionalist is not deprived of resources sufficient to his or her perceived needs.

Tsimihety followed a way of allocating resources not so much equally as equitably (recognizing that the needs of individuals and their households differed). At the same time they regulated their political affairs, the affairs of the village (i.e., the polis), without the benefit of hierarchy, and they remained indifferent to wealth, and hence to economic inequality as we tend to understand it. This indifference was manifest, I think, in the absence of decoration or display or the accumulation of goods. This lack of aesthetic expression was what so puzzled me, for the emphasis was on function rather than form, on pure utility and no frills. However, as I have come to realize, this is not an entirely convincing argument. Tsimihety did possess wealth, and hence the possible means for inequality, in cattle. But before I examine this question I shall discuss first the management of land, the primary resource, and how it was distributed equitably and did not become the basis of property, status, or rank.

Of all the notions fundamental to the theory and practice of a consciously organized society, including traditional tribal as well as modern capitalist society, the idea of the ownership of property is central. For "individualist" theory, private property is the safeguard against coercion and hence a safeguard of freedom (Hayek 1960:140); "collectivist" theory sees private property as the instrument of coercion, especially of the owner over the worker. But while collectively owned property may ensure the freedom and equality of the individual, the idea that land must be circumscribed and managed for the collective still acknowledges property, inequality, and confinement. Though there was a sense of circumscription among Tsimihety, it was not, I shall argue, as finely drawn and physical as to constitute property based on a right of exclusion.

Androna, as I have already stated, was a domain of influence rather than a bounded territory. Although the vast majority of people living there were Tsimihety, there were sizable minorities of other Malagasy, including some who had married Tsimihety. Though they were considered foreigners or guests, they were nevertheless settled, and Tsimihety life largely ignored them. Likewise the boundaries of the faritany were permeable, and within each faritany were many "types" (*karazana/foko*) of Tsimihety. The social boundaries of land—tanindrazana/zafintany—were radii of influence, not territorial frontiers. Tsimihety came and went, and they moved on, to the west, into Sakalava lands.

As far as I could ascertain by inference from Tsimihety practice and some discussion, Tsimihety ideas of what gave a person the right against others to use a piece of land was the continued investment of labor. The persons who cleared bush from a piece of land and who continued to keep it free from bush by slashing, burning, weeding, and planting were the persons who were entitled to the continued use of that land as against any other claimants. Tsimihety would certainly have agreed with John Locke that "labour, being the unquestionable property of the labourer, no man but he can have the right to what that is once joined to, at least where there is enough, and as good left in common for others" (Locke 1690/1952:para. 26). As far as the Tsimihety were concerned, what defined the tanindrazana was the fact that the ancestors in the tomb first cleared and cultivated the land and their ancestral labors of guardianship continued to constitute an investment in this particular land. All descendants of the first settlers had been responsible for keeping the land clear and in cultivation by their labors. By the same token land that had been once cleared but had since reverted to bush (*ambanivohitra*) was land that was "free."

But whereas Locke, by his definition, identified private property, Tsimihety would, by the same definition, deny the privacy of property, at least in land. It was the *continuing* input of labor by those whose identities were attached by ascent, that defined tanindrazana. No individual could claim exclusive rights because no individual had made an exclusive contribution. Tanindrazana "belonged" to the ancestors, who were still active, as well as to the living, so there was no way the living could alienate land. Tsimihety could give permission to vahiny to cultivate the land, but they could not, and would not, sell land outright. That is, vahiny, by asking permission, were in fact agreeing to keep land in use *on behalf of* Tsimihety, not instead of them.

Within the tanindrazana not every square meter of land was under cultivation all the time, but this did not mean that someone else could take this land away by cultivating it. Land within the faritany was allocated annually (see p. 48), and land that was not in use could be reallocated by the zafintany. But if land had been allowed to stand idle for such a time as to be deemed abandoned, it could be taken over. The problem here was to decide what period of time constituted abandonment. Such quarrels over land that did occur revolved around this problem, and I shall have more to say on this later.

The staple food of Tsimihety was rice (*vary*); indeed, as is common in different parts of the world, the staple was equated with food, and the remaining comestibles were simply relishes and side dishes. Thus Tsimihety depended on rice fields for their subsistence. With but few exceptions dry rice, as opposed to irrigated rice, was grown. The annual crop was harvested and stored in granaries that formed the outer rows of villages. From a subsistence point of view, then, rice lands (*tanimbary*) were the most important. They were distributed as follows.

At some time in August members of a village or a cluster of villages and hamlets assembled as a formal gathering (*fokon'olona*). The gathering was presided over by the elders (*raymandreny*). Each household head was invited to comment on how well his harvest had gone (most people knew anyway), on how well his needs had been met, what his anticipated needs were for the following year, and how far present resources were adequate. Everyone, zafintany and vahiny alike, was invited to have their say. The reply was usually embroidered with graphic accounts of the problems of the previous year—bad luck with vermin, inconsiderate neighbors whose bunding of their rice fields could have been more careful, or whose cattle could have been led through more considerately, and so on. No opportunity was lost to point out to everyone how much hard work had been put in. Though the meeting (*kabary*) was formally convened it was conducted in a good spirit without any pedantry over procedure. The main point was to assess the changing needs of households and the changing state of the soil so that land for cultivation could be reallocated between households and to fallow. The decisions were made by the elders, the senior generation plus, in many instances, the "chef de village." But it was a decision discussed and arrived at in public and with contributory suggestions made by everybody present, male and female, old or newly married. Thus there was no wholesale redistribution of land every year, and in any given sequence of years one set of fields might be kept continuously in cultivation for several seasons. People were not necessarily equal in terms of acreage possessed or used, but everyone was given equal consideration by everyone else in terms of their estimated requirements. There was little chance of inflating these requirements because it was common knowledge how many people there were in each household. But overall, this was a mode

of distribution that provided no foundation for inequality, for the transformation of property in land for subsistence to property in land for
surplus that could be parlayed into wealth, and thence social inequality
and political power.

All this is strongly reminiscent of East African and Sudanese pastoralists. Among the Fur of the Sudan, for example,

> Every person who is recognized as a member of a Fur local com-
> munity has access to land. Land is administered by the local chief
> and is allocated to members of the community according to need.
> Usufruct rights can be exercised only as long as one cultivates the
> land. When land is laid fallow after a few years' cultivation, the
> farmer has no rights to it any longer; rights to reallocate revert to
> the chief. The farmer has no right to alienate his land. (Haaland
> 1969:62)

Having described the division and allocation of rice land as an
uncomplicated procedure I must now muddy the picture by noting variations. The first variation is conditionally inherited rice land known as
tanimbary lova or *zazalava*. I did not come across many examples of
this, but most people I discussed it with agreed it was a legitimate custom.
Tanimbary lova were rice fields that had been continuously cultivated
for several years, or generations even, at the behest of the ancestor who
first cleared and planted the land. Usually this was land of exceptional
quality (river silt, for example) or land that was irrigated. As long as
the land was kept in cultivation by the man's patrilineal descendants,
or their nominees (usually maternal relatives or affines), then tanimbary
lova were not available for reallocation among zafintany.

By the same token the people who cultivated this land would not
put in for other land in the faritany, or if they did, they probably would
not get any unless they needed it. Tanimbary lova could be allowed to
remain fallow, but it had to be clear that it was "being kept alive"; as
soon as such land reverted to bush, or was evidently not being cared
for, it became part of the pool available for reassignment. Exclusive
hereditary right to rice land was possible among Tsimihety, but it was
conditional and restricted and, until 1963, had not threatened the ideal
of equity.

But when did "inherited" land that was not being used cease to be
exclusive or "private" property? When did an overgrowth become vacant

bush? Did rights simply fade away, or did they die at a specific point? For obvious reasons Tsimihety kept away from courts, but on an odd occasion when they had to go to court, the resulting record provided a case that brings principles to light.

At the village of Ankavankibo, a few kilometers from Ankiabe Salohy and situated in the same tanindrazana, Rafahetra had "inherited" as zazalava about two hectares of rice fields from his father. His father had actually been the first person to clear the land from bush and cultivate it and he had announced in front of the fokon'olona that he wanted this piece of land to be zazalava. Rafahetra had helped his father to cultivate the land, but soon after he got married he left for Tananarive where he was educated and became a civil servant. All his children were born in Tananarive and most had grown up there. After twenty-seven years away Rafahetra returned to Anka-vankibo where he expected, and then insisted, on his right to resume cultivation of his two hectares. Rafahetra was now in his mid-fifties.

About five years after he had left the village, the fokon'olona had allotted some of the paddy land to other people of the village, since Rafahetra had not designated anyone to cultivate on his behalf. Since this was rich riverine soil the land had been kept in constant cultivation, so when he came back Rafahetra saw everything ready made and ordered the present cultivators off. These people refused arguing that since Rafahetra had abandoned the land he had no right to it as tanimbary lova. He put no work into it to keep it alive, and the fokon'olona agreed with them.

Rafahetra, though born Tsimihety, was an indoctrinated civil servant, so he went to court in Mandritsara. The judge happened to be Merina. The court found for Rafahetra and instructed the villagers to return him his land without delay. The elders, on return-ing to the village, refused to accept this verdict, arguing that by going to Tananarive and not designating someone to keep the land alive, Rafahetra had signalled his intention to allow the land to return to bush, i.e., to return it to the zafintany. The village waited for several years, just in case, but when the bushes reached near shoulder height, all had agreed it was vacant. So they cleared it again and allocated it.

Rafahetra responded by going to Mandritsara and returning with two gendarmes, one of whom was Tsimihety from Bealanana who refused to do anything. When they left, villagers, including his close kinfolk, made life so difficult for Rafahetra (they ignored him socially, they heckled him if he tried to speak, they walked away from him, they refused to donate any labor to help rebuild his house, and they refused to supply him with any rice—he had to buy it from the Merina trader in Kalandy), that after a few weeks he left to go back to Tananarive.

Compared to English or American systems of land tenure, which would have allowed Rafahetra to return to "his" land, even after a twenty-seven year absence, Tsimihety clearly did not allow individual "ownership," and the concept underlying their attitude considered individuals as stewards whose responsibility was to manage the land on behalf of the ancestors. While they did so they were entitled to their subsistence. But "ownership" was not so much possession as unbroken association over time. It was not a collective ownership as we understand it, but a collective stewardship perhaps. Such a relationship, among other things, clearly facilitates the seminomadism of Tsimihety.

Whereas tanimbary lova at first suggests an exception to the rule that land cannot be privately owned or transmitted, *tanimbary omby* suggests an exception to the "rule" that land was allocated equitably. This was land that was used deliberately to produce a surplus of rice. It was any area of a faritany than was allotted to an individual, or kinship group, or the entire village over and above their subsistence needs. Its cultivation was conditional upon the offering of cattle to the ancestors and a feast to the living, and it was brought into use for reasons such as the following. If a man or a group of kin (usually brothers) knew that they would have unusual demands coming up, such as a marriage feast or an offering, or to pay taxes, then the fokon'olona and rayamandreny would be asked for permission to cultivate tanimbary omby. If the village as a whole or any segment of it found its rice stocks low because of unexpected demands (funeral meals, for instance, or excessive destruction by vermin), it might seek to rebuild future stocks by requesting to cultivate tanimbary omby. The case for such cultivation had to be made before the fokon'olona, i.e., every adult resident, but it was decided by the senior men of the zafintany. A decision in favor was not a foregone conclusion. Apart from the merits of the submission it had to be ascertained whether the extra labor would be available. Whoever made tanimbary omby had to "hire" labor by providing meals with meat and, sometimes, alcohol. Attractive though this was, people had to decide if they would have enough time to spare from working their own fields. Tanimbary omby, then, was a contingency category of land, not one that would allow individuals to cultivate in order to produce a surplus which could be used to their social, political, or economic ambitions. And finally, though tanimbary omby is a category well-known throughout Androna, it was not one posessed or recognized by all foko, so it was not actually found everywhere.

Taking any one faritany over a period of time, the pressure on its land varied over the years, depending on population and ecological conditions (rainfall, successful fallowing, flooding, overcropping, vermin plagues). Sometimes the amount of rice land available may have been too little; sometimes there would be more than enough. Most Tsimihety kept an informal record of conditions in Androna, particularly of conditions in those areas where they had close kinship connections. In addition, given the low population density of the region as a whole, there were still vacant areas that could be opened up by homesteaders. Thus, there was a constant shifting around that occurred on an individual, household basis rather than as any sort of mass movement, and the lines along which these shifts were made were usually kinship connections.

The connection that was given first priority was that between a father and his son, which, by cumulating this affiliation, became a connection of patrilineal ascent (*fokondraiky/fokondray*). Zafintany, ideally, were the patrilineal descendants of the ancestors or those who had first title to be buried in the tomb. But, if one's mother had access to good land, or available land, through her paternal connections, it was possible to keep these alive and active by going to live in her tanindrazana with the status *fokondreny*. In some cases this could be made permanent, for if a man came to be buried in his mother's tomb, his sons would be buried in "his" tomb, i.e., fokondraiky. Another way of gaining access to land, less desirable but widely practiced nevertheless, was to live *jaloko,* in the tanindrazana of one's wife, where she would be entitled to cultivate land through her father. The social position of a man who lived jaloko was marginal and underprivileged, but he swallowed his pride and, in time, he and especially his children could become well-established.

Thus as far as rice land was concerned there was a definite framework for access and distribution that took equity and security as its basic premises, and which defined a universal right: that every individual was guaranteed access to land wherever he or she was zafintany. Although there was an order of priority, it was not an order of privilege that could be exploited to lead to inequalities. Underlying the social framework governing land use was the fact that the entire region inhabited by Tsimihety and surrounding them was underpopulated and so allowed room for expansion.

Population pressure on rice fields was rarely cited to me as a reason for moving. It may be that, objectively, there was such pressure, but that was not how Tsimihety saw it. They saw pressure on pastures as far more real and recurring.

Pastures (*kijany*) were situated on the hillsides, along the ridges, and in the valleys where, and when, the land was not in use for rice and vegetable cultivation. Cattle were invariably brought in to graze the rice stubble after the harvest. Pastures were mostly within the boundaries of the faritany, but they also spilled into the no-man's-land between faritany and often it was easy to poach into neighboring faritany. Pastures remained undivided, and all the cattle of the villages roamed the pastures under the care of young boys. However, there was an informal rule of politeness that allowed cattle belonging to the older men of a village to pasture their cattle closer to the village. This meant that others had to go farther afield. If the journey to and from the pastures got too long and prevented adequate grazing, it was time to seek greener pastures. Cattle taken too far away so that they had to spend nights as well as days away from the village became easy targets for rustling, and this affected younger cattle owners in particular.

As will be gathered, cattle were brought back to the village corral each evening by their owners or the owner's herdboy. That is, although cattle were grazed over undivided pastures they were always kept in their herds. Cattle were corralled together at night, and in the morning were sorted out into their respective herds, which were then driven separately to pasture. So, although there were collective aspects of cattle rearing, individual ownership was never lost sight of, and I shall discuss this individualism and ownership in the following chapter.

Though the pastures were open, the "trespassing" of one owner's herd upon the pasture of another was a frequent complaint. The general informal rule, as I have indicated, was that seniors pasture closer to the village than juniors and seniors also claimed first priority to richer pastures. These "rules" were very vague, as were the definitions of "better" pastures, and since complaints were made on the basis, usually, of reports made by children, they were very inconclusive and generally constituted a continuing, but unresolvable, source of grumbling in a village or between villages. This, as far as I could tell, was as much a reason as any for making people, especialy younger ones, move on. However, since cattle were the focus of Tsimihety ideas corresponding to our ideas about wealth and a difference of talents, I must allow the possibility that there were genuine pressure tactics involved in pasture usage that resulted in withdrawals and migrations.

Though rice was synonymous with food and thence with subsistence in Tsimihety opinion, there were a variety of crops cultivated, and the land so used was specifically identified and allocated independently of rice fields. First in importance, from an outsider's point of view, were the vegetable gardens (*taninanana*), though from Tsimihety points of view they were hardly worth talking about. There were men's gardens in which were grown varieties of *ovy* or yams, manioc, maize, beans, and banana; and women's gardens in which were grown a wide variety of leaf greens, legumes, cucurbits, onions, herbs, tomatoes, and the like. Manioc and maize did not rate a mention by Tsimihety as even edible, yet they were widely eaten to break fasts when granaries ran low, just before harvest. They were also eaten more or less year round as snacks. Ears of corn were often left roasting by the fire, and people helped themselves, while a pot of boiling manioc might be left over the fire all day, only being taken off when the rice was to be cooked. Yams, too, were eaten to break fasts and as snacks, but sometimes were eaten instead of rice. The gardens in which these crops were grown were usually situated away from the rice fields, on the edge of the tanindrazana and hidden in the bush, as befitted their marginal role. Not all households made such gardens, or rather not all admitted to doing so, and certainly they were invariably hidden from easy view. The husband/father was responsible for the garden and was helped by his sons, but such gardens were as often created and cultivated by brothers living in the same village together with their sons. Arrangements seemed to vary as to whether the jointly cultivated gardens were divided for use, or whether the garden remained undivided and used freely according to need. Permission to cultivate such gardens was not required, though people were generally informed they had been made. Nor were cleared gardens kept in continuous use over the years; in fact they quickly returned to bush, and there seemed to be no sense of them being transmitted from father to son.

In contrast to the informality of male gardens and their rather slapdash cultivation, women's gardens were carefully and intensively cultivated. Usually they were located just outside the village, close to running water and not too far from the corral, from which women took manure. Being heavily manured and well watered, these gardens tended to remain in use year after year and to remain clear of bush. They were laid out rather like an English allotment. Each household had one or more gardens measuring about 8×8 meters; gardens were divided into beds, each of which was planted with a particular vegetable. In principle each garden was controlled by the senior woman of the household, who supervised its cultivation. She was assisted by her daughters, no matter how young, and some mothers gave their daughters their own corner of a garden to cultivate for themselves. This was especially the case in villages near Mandritsara, where there was a daily market (patronized mostly by Tsimihety and non-Tsimihety civil service employees). Women sold vegetables here and used the money to buy such popular commodities as tins of Nestlés condensed milk, or cloth.

When a woman married, she usually went to live in her husband's village. Upon leaving her natal village she handed back her vegetable beds to her mother, and upon her arrival in the new village, received beds from her mother-in-law. If a new wife arrived and there was no vegetable garden for her, her husband was be expected to create one for her. If there was a divorce, the garden went (back) to the mother-in-law. Women's gardens were not inherited in the usual sense, but they were maintained in continuous use. I do not know what would happen if a mother refused to hand over a garden to her daughter-in-law or whether there was any "rule" that would be invoked and sanctions applied.

Though not a category of land, some trees had a special status as well as being economically important. Preeminent among these was the raphia palm, which was to Tsimihety what bamboo is to other Malagasy and to the people of Southeast Asia in general. Raphia (*fomby*) was used in building houses, making furniture, and weaving mats, baskets, and cloth, which, in turn, was used to make hats, winding sheets, and, less frequently in those days, waterproof clothing. Oil pressed from the nut was used for cooking while the inner lining of leaves was used as tobacco paper. Under the French regime, the growing and harvesting of raphia was encouraged, and statistics record a steady rise in production from 875 kilos of leaf in 1912 to 656 tonnes in 1962 in the district of Mandritsara. Raphia was a traditional crop, and the trees were considered to be under the jurisdiction of zafintany, who traditionally allocated on the basis of stated need. Making raphia a cash crop made for difficulties, however, and every effort was made to combat the tendency toward inequality this might foster. In some villages, at an approved time, all able-bodied men were given permission to harvest raphia, and the harvest was then divided in equal amounts among zafintany households. Sometimes vahiny households were given the same amounts; sometimes they received none at all. In other villages I found that individual households requested permission to harvest raphia as and when they needed it. They asked, or rather informed, the *soja* or the chef de village. In some villages all the adolescent males were given the go-ahead to shin up the trees and collect what they could; then the harvest was distributed according to request at a village meeting (kabary). Individuals who had come by raphia could sell, if they chose, just as they could sell rice—usually to itinerant Cormorian traders. But this was sold from their allocation rather than as a surplus.

In 1963 one could spot Tsimihety villages from a distance by the towering clumps of kapok trees that surrounded them. Kapok was introduced by the French in 1932 as a cash crop. In 1933, 100,000 kapok trees were planted, but reports speak of difficulties in getting the crop harvested, and in exporting what had been harvested. The highest production figure recorded was 26 tonnes in 1956. Tsimihety had little use for kapok trees, and they resorted to collecting it only when there was a financial emergency, like tax demands. There were no controls placed on the trees. In a few villages coffee was grown, and here the trees were individually owned. Some people, I believe, did sell the beans to merchants, but most seemed to be kept back for their own use and for barter trade.

The French also introduced certain fruits, including a particularly luscious variety of mango (*mango bory*), oranges, and pineapple. These were first grown from nursery seedlings and distributed to Tsimihety. Very few pineapples were grown, but the orange, grapefruit, and mango trees were regarded as being owned individually and could be handed on from father to son. The fruits were often handed to the women to sell, alongside their vegetables, in the market. Or they were eaten by the people themselves and given as gifts when visiting. Jackfruit trees were found in some villages, and these, too, were eaten by villagers. Other fruit trees and bushes, including plums, guava, mango, pomegranate, and varieties of berry are known collectively as *voasary gasy* and were gathered by any who wished. These crops were not intentionally cultivated, though they were appreciated, and were picked and sold in the market. Three highly prized products were obtained by Tsimihety through barter with the forest dwellers of the east. These were tobacco, honey, and, above all, salt. This was a vegetable salt produced by slowly reducing the inner bark of a tree to ash, which was then packed in leaves for transport and storage. Another vital resource, firewood, was collected by both men an women, adult and child, from the scrub and woodland patches throughout the region.

Lastly there was the relation of people to the village (*tanana*). As I have already hinted, it was the tomb rather than the settlement that was the focus and center defining people's place, their spatial identity, their sense of belonging. Villages were movable, hence temporary, and no great ritual, sentimental, or economic value was placed on them. They could be easily abandoned. This is not to say they had no significance. They were sited with great care and only after due consultation of the *sikidy* or divination system, as well as with the ancestors. Houses, too, were only built after due consultation, with time as well as site duly divined. So, while people were free to come and go, they were not free to build exactly when and where they wished.

Ideally a village was founded by a man, his household, and his junior, male kinsmen who collected around him. But since access to villages was free, nonkin or distant kin could as easily settle. However, when they did the village divided into sections (*fijarana*). There was no perceptible physical boundary between sections, but often each section had its own altar (*fijoroana*), the focus of activities directed toward ancestors, and was nucleated around a central household, with other households having close kin connections. The original settlers, who were usually zafintany in the faritany, were the *tompontanana* or seniors of the village. All subsequent settlers built southwest of them because seniority was spatially indicated by living to the northeast, the direction from which the ancestors were believed to have come. All villages, no matter what their size, had a settlement patten consisting of parallel rows of houses separated by "streets" with granaries on the periphery.

Houses were solidly built of mud, dung, and thatch around a wooden frame, and there were very few "old style" palm thatch huts to be found.

Most that were inhabited were lived in by those tromba who were unmarried women. There was usually one door, and inside sleeping and eating mats were hung on the walls when not in use. Some houses had a separate kitchen, while others had a hearth inside the main house. Privacy from neighbors was effective, but members of a household did not enjoy individual privacy. Etiquette respected this privacy, and the approach of a visitor was signalled with successive declamations of *Hôdy!* (anyone at home!). Entry was only after permission had been granted.

Although the labor involved in building a house was substantial, it was donated in a working bee at which the builder fed his helpers. In spite of this investment houses might be abandoned at the slightest pretext. It was no longer mandatory to abandon a house after a death, but I met no one who was willing to live in such a house. The compromise was that the house would not automatically be burned down, as used to be the case. Illness, bad luck, desire for new scenery or new neighbors, feeling like a change, desire to live nearer favorite relatives, anxiety at a crack that appeared in a wall, and wishing to live nearer to children who had gone to school in Mandritsara were among the reasons given to me for people's removal.

When a house was abandoned it was not necessarily left empty. It automatically became available as a village guest house for kin, missionaries, officials, or visiting anthropologists. Most commonly an empty house was used as a place where young unmarried people could entertain visitors of the opposite sex from other villages, in which case it became known as *kotravahy* (young men's house) or *kotravavy* (young women's house). Empty houses were also available for use by people wishing to return to the village as a stopgap dwelling before they built their own house. In other words, a house was a possession only when, and for as long as, it was in use. Once it had been vacated it was free for another occupant to take up tenancy. The principles guiding the relation of people to building land were the same as for their relation to rice land and to the tanindrazana in general: people had a right of use that stemmed from their relation to the tomb via their relation to zafintany. They enjoyed no right of ownership or possession. People were therefore free to leave without being detained by ties of individual property, just as they were guaranteed recognition, shelter, and land elsewhere where they were zafintany, or in a less secure sense as vahiny.

People did own personal, movable property, and every household possessed at least one of the large, cast-iron cooking pots that were hung over the fire and known by the French term *marmites*. Men owned tools (slashers, shovels, scythes, etc., all made by a local, Tsimihety black-smith), and often a suitcase; women owned utensils (plates, cutlery, pans), cloth, basins, chests, mats, lamps, trinkets, and some owned sewing machines. These items were all portable and were carried either in an ox cart or by porter to new places of residence. Such property was no impediment to mobility. Some people had raphia furniture that could either be transported or abandoned. Every senior man, who was *soja* and/or *mpijoro* (these terms are discussed in chapters 3 and 4), had a cane and was buried with his cane, hat, jacket, plate, and spoon.

Conclusion

Political freedom, freedom from the imposition of the will of those who claim superiority, is notoriously at risk among settled, agricultural people. Their commitment to land and their way of life weighs them down so that they find it difficult to escape. Agriculturalists in Africa or South Asia found it difficult to evade colonial invasions, while peasants the world over have found it difficult to escape the domination of the demands of urban centers. Such confinement often necessitates violence as a form of resistance. But this is less true of pastoralists who, seminomadic and self-contained in so many respects, are notoriously opposed in some way or other to attempts to dominate them and are often described as considering themselves superior to their neighbors and the rest of humankind. Many East African pastoralists live in small hamlets or scattered homesteads (e.g., Nandi) as do other Malagasy pastoralists such as the Bara. Little value is placed on crop cultivation, though crops are necessary for subsistence, so that some observers have remarked that such people may have no system of land tenure (such an official description of the Kipsigis is cited by Manners 1964:268). Some pastoralists do have chiefs, but others, like the Tsimihety, do not, and the significance of this for the difficulty of colonial administration was appreciated by Huntingford when writing of the Nandi (1953:15, 26).

Tsimihety were subsistence agriculturalists, at least to all appearances, depending upon the cultivation of rice. But they thought of themselves as pastoralists. Cattle came first in their scheme of values, and this would seem to be correlated in a functional sense with their political views. The necessities of pastoralism provided them with an objectification of values that constituted and supported their desire for liberty.

The big difference between Tsimihety and other pastoralists was their pacifist attitude. Ever since the Merina state set about incorporating them, Tsimihety have with considerable success maintained a high degree of political liberty, first against the Merina, then against the French, and finally against the first national republican government. Unlike some other Malagasy people, and many other people in different parts of the world, they have done so without resorting either to overt or guerrilla violence and without developing a politically schizophrenic life—in which they obeyed their colonial masters in the daytime and in the evening followed the dictates of their own, alternative political structure, somewhat in the way described by Althabe for the Betsimisaraka. Tsimihety, in other words, achieved their freedom without cost to their integrity. In this chapter I have outlined what I consider the basic material conditions that have made this possible.

Undoubtedly the first of these was the relative emptiness of the mid-northern region of Madagascar, which Tsimihety moved into and continue to move across. This emptiness made mobility easy, either as a long-term creeping across the landscape or as a short-term evasive tactic. Upon the approach of suspicious-looking strangers, people would vanish from a village and hide out in the hills, still during my stay. The ability to move away and around made any sort of administration difficult at a grass-roots level, hence difficult for an external government to impose its will. Tactics of avoidance were developed by Tsimihety in response to Merina military oppression over a number of years in the nineteenth century, and I am not suggesting they were deliberately contrived as a rational strategy.

Granted the fundamental, and possibly necessary, natural conditions, the sustaining of this freedom and independence depended very much on the attitude developed by Tsimihety toward land and its resources. It was a plain fact that everyone invested considerable labor in production for a delayed return. Though there was some hunting (for game such as fruit bats, lemurs, guinea fowl, wild cats, and rodents) and fishing (for fish such as tilapia) it was as a sport, and was by no means a substantial contribution to subsistence (though overall the eating of game was an important source of protein in Tsimihety diet). This investment was acknowledged, but not in the form of individual or even collective ownership of property. It was acknowledged as the means of establishing or continuing a right to use defined tracts of land (tanin-drazana) at any time. And this right was legitimized and stabilized in the tomb. The original ancestors cleared the land and put it to use; their descendants continued to keep the land alive, and one's contemporaries were engaged in preserving the life of the land. Rights were defined through ascent. But even if the land was not actively cultivated, the presence of a tomb meant the ancestors continued their work of guardianship and spiritual care. So if one was a descendant one could claim the right. Cultivation and propitiation were the duties that kept the land alive. Living people in any given generation may come and go from their tanindrazana, but the tomb and its inhabitants remain to permanently occupy the land. There was no way, then, in which the living could sell or otherwise dispose of land, since no individual(s) could ever identify themselves as sole proprietors. They may allow others to use the land, temporarily, but it could never leave their jurisdiction. Conversely, any individual who was zafintany could leave his tanindrazana without ever abandoning it, no matter how long he was away. The nomadic tendencies of Tsimihety were anchored in security. The material form of this anchor was the tomb, which, unlike the tombs of other Malagasy such as Merina, Betsileo, and others, was not a striking visible presence on the landscape. Tombs were secret, hidden, and unadorned centers as natural as the land and the hills of which they were a part. They cannot be easily interfered with by outsiders by even being gazed upon.

Tanindrazana were not exclusive territories. Outsiders (vahiny) were easily admitted as guests, often long-staying ones. But they did not become zafintany, unless by intermarriage and subsequent descent. However, being a vahiny in one place did not interfere with one's zafintany status elsewhere. Here the flexibility of descent and affiliation as criteria of admission needs to be mentioned, though it will be discussed in detail in chapter 4. The determination of who shall be buried in which tomb, and therefore who shall have rights of use as zafintany, was made by using patrifiliation as a rule of thumb. Ideally this aggregated into patrilineal ascent (or cumulative kinship, as described by Southall 1986). But though this rule applied in the majority of cases (at least those about which I have information), this was not a cast-iron rule, and membership could be granted on the basis of maternal and, more rarely, affinal relations. There were some cases where a man of another Malagasy group (but not Merina) was granted burial in his Tsimihety wife's tomb and his children established as zafintany.

Each case was determined on its merits, and the "rules" generally applied more as guidelines than as imperatives. Such flexibility contributed to the mobility of Tsimihety, for it meant that spiritually as well as physically they could always belong wherever they may be, so long as they remained within the orbit of fomba Tsimihety, Tsimihety tradition.

This willingness to be free and open to each other was, among other factors, the distinguishing feature that differentiated Tsimihety from outsiders, both Europeans and other Malagasy. It allowed for considerable individualism and in no way provided a structural basis for collectivism. Tsimihety were not a political or territorial organization opposed to outsiders; they were individuals who shared common sympathies with each other, including a sympathy for opposition against outside domination, and they were people who subscribed to a common management style of access to necessary subsistence resources. They emphasized equity of use, prevention of the use of land as a source of wealth, distribution of a sense of "ownership" or belonging through all time, in which the division between the dead and the living was a slow fading one and never absolute, and the materialization of these "values" in the tangible reality of the tomb.

Appendix

One of the many things that both irritated and puzzled me was the lack of any cuisine among Tsimihety. Their diet was straight out boring as far as I was concerned and, instead of meals being something to look forward to, they became something I dreaded. Like all rice-eating people, Tsimihety equated rice with food: if you had not eaten rice that day, you simply had not eaten. Rice was eaten two or three times a day: in the morning it was either leftover rice heated up or freshly boiled, but in both cases it was served watery. When special visitors, such as anthropologists, were present, it was sometimes served with Nestlés condensed milk, a universal favorite among Tsimihety and just about the only Western product approved without reservation. At midday rice was eaten with a relish of vegetables, all plain boiled, though some women added oil and chili to the vegetables. An evening meal seemed optional and was the same as the midday meal. When any visitor arrived from another village a chicken would be caught, defeathered, and boiled to be served with the rice. It was tough and gristly and a torture to eat, and I was unable to eat chicken for years and years after leaving Tsimihety. If it was just someone popping in, a chicken would not be killed or presented. If a visitor from afar or someone important arrived between meals, or could not stay for a meal, he or she was presented with a basket of uncooked rice and a live chicken. Chickens were kept in every village but neither they nor the eggs were eaten regularly. Game such as fruit bats, civet cat, and lemur were eaten if and when they were caught, but beef was eaten only on the occasion of a celebration or an offering. Cattle were certainly not kept for meat, or milk for that matter, since very few people milked cows. Milk was sold in the market or supplied to Europeans in Mandritsara, but Tsimihety rarely drank milk, or blood, or ate meat.

Tsimihety ate, of course, and snacked a great deal between meals on roasted corn, roasted insects (children in particular roasted beetles, grasshoppers, and grubs), guinea fowl, and fruit. But they seemed quite disinterested in what they were eating—everything was consumed as a matter of course without expressing any appreciation or contentment. This is not surprising considering how bland and completely unimaginative their cooking was. It was, however, consistent with their apparent lack of interest in other arts, such as decoration, ornament, music making, weaving, pottery, carving, metalwork, and the like. The women did weave on small back looms with raphia cloth, but only as and when they needed to and without any design on the cloth. They made baskets with a minimum design, did not make pottery, and the blacksmiths produced only purely functional artifacts on demand. Compared to all the reports from other Malagasy people, Tsimihety were aesthetically impoverished. And even if they indulged in no indigenous cuisine, boiling everything, using no spices but an occasional dash of chili and salt, it is surprising that a people colonized by the French remained so indifferent. Nor were they any more imaginative when it came to drink. The most common everyday drink was *ranompango*—water added to the pot after all the rice but the crust had been removed and then allowed to boil so as to take the flavor of the burnt rice. In a few villages some people grew coffee, but they knew little about roasting it. It was left to sun dry and was then coarsely ground. Most Tsimihety did not drink alcohol, but some villages produced sugarcane from which a fermented rum (*betsabetsa*) was produced and, more rarely, a distilled rum (*laoka*). This was bartered and used as much for addressing the ancestors (it was poured on the ground) as it was for drinking. A few villages closer to the forest fermented honey and made a sort of mead. Villagers living near Mandritsara sometimes bought French wine.

Tsimihety were uniformly well-nourished, at least as far as I could tell. They were fit and energetic and I do not recall ever seeing a fat person, let alone an obese one. During the course of a day, men, women, and children would, for one reason or another, walk several kilometers to rice fields, gardens, and pastures, to collect firewood or to visit friends and relatives.

Apart from condensed milk they had not taken to any European food—partly, I suspect, because these could only be bought with cash and Tsimihety avoided cash whenever they could. But, from my point of view, their lack of appreciation for what could be done with the food available to them was, first, a source of nausea to me, and second, a symptom of the plain straightforwardness of Tsimihety. This, I have come to appreciate, is all part of the necessary condition of their political life, which strives for independence and liberty from external dictate.

CHAPTER 3

Egalité

In the first chapter I discussed various possibilities that might explain the origin of the term *Tsimihety* and the approximate times and events which could be associated with the emergence of Tsimihety. These had to do in particular with the nature of the relations between certain people (those who became Tsimihety) and others (outsiders who tried to assume, or were placed in positions of, authority over them). These explanations were put forward in a context of an evolving resistance to domination, which threatened taken-for-granted liberty. There is, however, another possible explanation that takes its shape from the proposition that liberty and independence are best maintained (though not originally secured) by a political and moral condition of equality.

As I explained in chapter 1 the earlier population of Androna seems to have been composed of relatively small organizations under the leadership of relatively weak chiefs, or, in some cases, stronger mpanjaka. The record of their opposition against Merina invasion is one of continued failure either to keep the Merina out or to defeat them. At one point this failure was so widespread and shared by so many of these small political groups that a number of chiefs allegedly committed suicide. Though they did not try to resist the French militarily, Tsimihety came to similar grief in that they were rid of the Merina only to find themselves dominated even more effectively by the French (and Sakalava agents). Although some Tsimihety may have participated in military contest with the French, they did not succeed. What actually failed in the nineteenth century against outsiders was organized or group resistance. Let us call these smallish groups "bodies." These bodies were political structures organized around hierarchies, albeit weak ones. As structures they suffered corporate defeat, and as organizations most of them lost their heads, their chiefs. Normally new heads "grow" or are appointed according to descent priorities in these sorts of structures, but for reasons I shall discuss below, defeat, and possibly dispersal, meant that the chiefs were not succeeded and because of this the organizations faded. Thus the attributes that were Tsimihety were summed up in the meaning of the term, i.e., those who did not cut their hair, which meant those who observed no hierarchy, which meant those who shared the attributes of not living in structures built around hierarchies. Tsimihety meant that set of people who, for common historical reasons of invasion, failure, and evasion, shared the attribute of having devolved from a (weak) hierarchical political structure to an egalitarian one. This was enough to provide a mass of people with a common sentiment of being of one kind; in fact, it closely parallels John Stuart Mill's strongest specification for the feeling of nationality:

> Geographical limits are one of its causes. But the strongest of all is identity of political antecedents, collective pride and humiliation, pleasure and regret, connected with the same incidents in the past. (Mill 1952 [1861]:424)

To say Tsimihety is a set does not mean that no organization was to be found among Tsimihety, that they were totally anarchic and anomic, like the unfortunate Ik; it does not mean that they were as freewheeling as hunter/gatherers and could operate without prejudice as self-sufficient individuals should they wish to do so. But whatever organizations existed must not threaten to take over, or subvert, the Tsimihety set by converting it into a political organization. And this was not just a political fact, but a matter of theory. That is to say, the principle of an effective political hierarchy was outlawed among Tsimihety, and only restricted, specialized, functional, and nonconvertible hierarchies were recognized. Tsimihety life was organized and structured *within* the set, but in accordance with the condition of set membership—that each and every individual was an equal and was not ranked. How this condition of equality existed relative to the organization of affairs, especially of work and wealth and frictions, is what I shall attempt to reconstruct from my fieldnotes, without any expectation that I can provide a full and satisfactory reconstruction, or that Tsimihety met this condition with perfection. I expect they were as fallible as anyone else.

Rice and Labor

Rice was the basis of subsistence, but there was a small market in Mandritsara and Befandriana for rice, as well as constant demand from other centers such as Majunga. Itinerant merchants, mostly Cormorian, maintained a steady, though not insistent, demand for rice such that selling rice was the easiest way for Tsimihety to acquire cash should they need to do so. Having to pay a tax was the main reason why Tsimihety wanted cash, but other reasons included making up a *moletry* or bridewealth, a *meomeo* or dowry, buying cloth, and occasionally imported hardware such as enamel bowls, cutlery, and crockery. Sewing machines, which could be seen in a number of houses, were usually acquired by a woman and/or her brother going off to work, usually in Majunga, specifically to earn money for a machine.

There was, then, some pressure on Tsimihety to engage in the cash economy, though for most of them, it was only in a piecemeal and marginal sense. Tsimihety who wished to pass from the subsistence/barter economy into the cash economy proper usually had to leave Androna. Individuals who did so were not hindered or penalized, but every effort was made to keep the cash economy out of Tsimihety, not least by the allocation of rice land on a subsistence need basis, on the regular reassessment of these needs, and on the tacit surveillance implied in this mode of allocation. By shutting out the cash economy Tsimihety closed off outside influence and a major opening for social hierarchy founded on wealth.

Concomitantly, claims to individual (or even collective) ownership of land were blocked, as we have discussed. The effective limit on access to land was the labor that individuals, or small groups, could recruit to bring it into production and, more importantly, keep it alive so that they could maintain exclusive access to it. If individuals could somehow gain access to land from which they could produce surplus grain, they could then produce wealth. The principal means for gaining such access would be the ability to command the labor of others, or the ability to control a division of labor especially through technology. If, for example, some individuals used ploughs and tractors while others carried on with traditional methods, or even if too many people went over to wet rice farming, they could acquire a surplus that, upon sale for cash, could be translated into wealth and status. I am not suggesting that Tsimihety knew in any rational or theoretical sense that technology would produce surplus or that entering the cash economy would convert them into a status system or even a class system. What they *did* know quite explicitly was that relying on cash would bring to an end fomba Tsimihety and tie them too closely with government (fanjakana) and the outside world

in the persons of traders, administrators who granted licenses, and functionaries who collected taxes. What I as a Western member of a capitalist
society reckon was that the end of fomba Tsimihety meant class and
hierarchy via cash and wealth. If Tsimihety didn't know these specifics
or work to them consciously they would, I think, have nodded their
heads vigorously in agreement if I had suggested this. Here, then, was
the connection between liberty and equality for the Tsimihety—that if
they changed from their subsistence economy and its details to a cash
economy based on wealth, they would get trapped into external domination by entering into hierarchical, status relations among themselves
and, in a continuum, with outsiders.

Thus, the details of Tsimihety production of rice, particularly the
organization of labor set within a context of the relation to land discussed
in the previous chapter, could be shown to be a, if not the, raison d'être
of the means to achieve such ends as the preservation of a subsistence
economy against the encroachments of a cash economy. In turn, this
may be understood as a means to preserve and keep functional an
egalitarian outlook on daily life.

Villages were small, on average about forty people in about ten to
twelve households. The household was the unit of most activity—a household ate and slept together and was responsible for the production of
its own subsistence needs. Submissions for land needs were made by the
household head for his household, and allocation was made on the
estimate of the household's needs. But household composition varied
according to the life cycle: young children, adolescents, no children, old
people, a preponderance of females or males, and various mixtures. This
meant that a household's productive capabilities were variable in that
sometimes it had more than enough labor to produce for its needs, and
sometimes it did not have enough to perform the tasks involved in rice
production. These tasks were clearing (male, or male and female if
burning); trampling (male); bunding (male, but could use female assistance); broadcasting (male, occasionally female); guarding against birds
and vermin (female, children, occasionally male); harvesting (male);
stacking, threshing, winnowing (female, but males drove cattle for threshing); and storing (female). In wet rice cultivation women transplanted
seedlings.

I knew some examples of households that did all these tasks of
production themselves. I knew of one case where a brother and sister
lived together and not only cultivated their own fields but helped others

out. But most people joined forces with other households to form a specially designated work group (*asareky*). Small villages usually made up one work group, but larger villages had several groups that in many cases coincided with the spatial division of the village into sections (*fijarana*). Not always, though. In many cases asareky looked to be organized on the basis of cooperation between households cultivating contiguous fields irrespective of where they lived in the village. There was nothing formal about asareky in that they did not have a permanent place in any organization and were not themselves structured groups. Each year the men and women of village households mentioned, during the course of conversations, getting together in asareky. Agreement to do so was on the tacit, but strict, understanding that the able-bodied members of each household would work for one day on each others' rice land. This day-to-day reciprocity continued until all the necessary work was done. The setting up of a work group was, then, spontaneous, though the idea of doing so was Tsimihety custom. Composition varied each year, and much depended on the state of relations between people at the time because there was a strong element of voluntarism, hence trust, involved. It so happened that, because of the way in which small villages and fijarana were settled, asareky were for the most part kin, usually centered around brothers or a father and his adult sons. But asareky were not recruited on that principle—kin were notoriously as likely to be on bad terms for short periods and, therefore, not to be trusted. The organization and direction of the asareky, as well as its sustenance, changed each day as the household whose fields were being worked assumed responsibility. Since an asareky was reciprocal and undertook to stick together for the single agricultural year, it placed some constraint on any intention to migrate. The timing of most departures was after harvest, though with some understanding on the part of one's workmates that arrangements could be made to suit.

There was one modification invariably found: the preparation of the rice fields by driving cattle around and around to churn them into mud (*magnosy*) was carried out on a village-wide basis, or, sometimes, on a several-villages-wide basis. This was because it was a favorite task for the young men; in fact, it was more of a sport. Cattle belonging to the households were brought together and taken from field to field by the young men, who rode and wrestled the animals and enjoyed themselves in the mud.

Households in an asareky whose labor contribution was less than that of the others had to make up the deficiency, which they did by employing the asareky, and/or any other able bodies and willing workers. To do so was known as *tambirô,* the term given to the "payment" that had to include meat or poultry and often rum (betsabetsa, the fermented rather than the distilled cane juice). Tambirô was also the way in which people could recruit labor to help them produce a small surplus to sell for an acceptable purpose such as paying taxes, or providing for a wedding.

I can only say that my impression is that this system of allocation and joint production seemed to provide roughly the amount of rice required by people, little more, and sometimes not enough. Merchants, urban residents, and officials complained to me that there was not enough rice produced and most of the rice for sale was imported from Befandriana. On the other hand, official statistics for 1954 indicate a total rice production for the District of Mandritsara of 33,537 tonnes, of which 2,096 tonnes were "exported." How these figures were arrived at I cannot say. I can see that the export figure could be accurately measured from merchants accounts, but the total figure must be pure guesswork because I am absolutely sure that neither officials nor Tsimihety weighed their crops, though Cormorian traders did, roughly.

Several varieties of rice were grown. These included *roaka, vato, kimoza, kiriminy, tsipala, madinika, lava,* and *mena kely.* Kiriminy and lava were "good quality" grains, being light, dry, and fragrant when cooked. They were introduced by the French and much appreciated by Tsimihety. But they were relatively slow growing and best grown in seedling beds, which was not the Tsimihety way. The great bulk of the rice grown was vary roaka, which was not a good-quality rice but which did not require too much care and gave a good yield. Most households, then, ate the same rice, even though it was not the preferred one. The better grains were reserved for visitors and, if possible, for ritual meals. Because a household did not grow the preferred grains, or very many of them, they often bought them from the merchants. Thus, what was seen sometimes by outsiders as an inability of Tsimihety to grow enough rice may often only have been a sign that their quality calculations were out that year.

Without being able to produce any statistics, either overall or for specific households, there is nothing that I noted which would lead me to think otherwise than that, in normal years, the arrangements for rice production were well-calculated and adequate. For me to have attempted

to measure, or even to be seen calculating, amounts of paddy in a
field, rice in a granary, or amounts consumed would have aroused and
confirmed Tsimihety suspicions that I was an agent of government
(fanjakana)—one who was out to boost an economy based on cash,
figures, and precise amounts, one who wanted a surplus to convert to
cash. Other than making *very* approximate calculations of acreage and
estimates of population, I made no effort toward a quantitative study.

Rice and rice land, the basis of subsistence, were also the substance
of Tsimihety property, if we understand property in its simplest Lockean
sense—the mixing of the labor of one's body with the earth. Tsimihety
also followed the Lockean precept of not producing more than they
needed; thus, land and rice were not potential foundations for surplus
and hence wealth, which might lead to an economically and eventually
a socially nonegalitarian society. Both the means of production (land)
and the relations of production were so arranged as to assure equitable
distribution.

Cattle

To some extent I think I was brainwashed by Tsimihety, both by what
they chose to tell me and, probably more to the point, what they did
not tell me, and by what I observed and what I did not see. I have been
puzzled for many years by people's apparent lack of interest in, and
concern for, the idea of anything beautiful. Tsimihety seemed to have
no aesthetic dimension to their lives. This seemed consistent with flat
egalitarianism—this disinterest in decoration and ornament, with lack
of attachment to place, and contentment with an even-keeled economy—
rather than a society rich in highs and lows of crops and symbols. In
a word, while Tsimihety understood property, they seemed to have no
sympathy with the idea of wealth—in the sense of abundance, surplus,
profusion, and display. Houses were plain and functional, tombs were
hidden, rituals were sparse and trimmed, entertainments were without
decoration—no one dressed up (except the bride at a wedding)—music
was rare and little more than percussive, oratory was peremptory.

To an anthropological reader it may seem naive to the point of
stupidity that I did not recognize in Tsimihety cattle the source of all
Tsimihety ideas, values, and practices of wealth. But I considered myself
to have lived with an agricultural people, rice farmers who also kept
cattle. I had heard Europeans deride Tsimihety for their attitude to cattle,

but I took this as part frustration, part truth. Tsimihety did seem to think more of, and about, cattle than raising their standard of living. What is more, Tsimihety said the same thing themselves without the tone of ridicule present in the attitude of vazaha. Another factor was that my own attitude to cattle, part personal, part cultural, was one that lacked sympathy for them as anything but meat on the hoof. I personally do not particularly like animals in the sense of having any affinity for them, so although I could see Tsimihety had a special attachment to cattle, it never dawned on me, because it was outside my range of sympathy, that cattle were wealth, riches, display, art, and, in general, the fountainhead of their aesthetic life. Only as I see myself as an unsympathetic observer do I realize what I missed so much of while I was among them. It is only as I contemplate what I wrote at the time, what I did not write, what I remember, and the picture the fieldwork as a whole has suggested to me, do I now realize, or at least consider, that understanding cattle as unconvertible wealth is the answer. Though considered wealth, cattle were not for sale. In a jigsaw puzzle, one is given a picture on the lid of the box and the task is, of course, to fit together the pieces inside the box to reproduce the picture on the cover. Notes, drafts, intuitions, and inferences have given me the picture "on the lid," and now I propose to put together the pieces to make the segment of the whole picture occupied by cattle.

First, as usual, a caution. Tsimihety were suspicious of any sign of someone measuring—land, crops, population, and, especially, cattle. Louis Molet, the principal ethnographer of Tsimihety, found the same resistance and defensiveness. He writes:

> Toujours, dans les villages, les questions concernant le nombre des boeufs excitent le mefiance et ne recoivent que les reponses evasives, approximatives ou même ouvertment erronée. (Molet 1953:48)

Molet's own study was based almost entirely on official statistics, but his own comment must throw doubt on their validity, for Tsimihety were no more willing to divulge accurate information about cattle to officials than they were to anthropologists. Their caution was not just because they were afraid of the consequences of reporting numbers and sizes, it was also that they did not attach much importance to numbers for their own purposes. They recognized, of course, that the opposite was true of governments, and to give such information only rebounded on them in the form of taxes and the like. But, for what they are worth, and to give a vague idea of the number of cattle in the District of Mandritsara, because American readers in particular want to know the scale of things, the number of cattle "registered" was as follows:

1960	1961	1962
126,275	129,098	119,944

This works out at roughly twice as many cattle as people, which compared with a national ratio of three to one. No figures of export or slaughter were recorded for the above years, but in 1959 there was recorded a total of 133,981 cattle, of which 4,871 were sent out of Mandritsara and 2,018 were recorded as having been slaughtered in the district, for which licenses were issued. The lack of figures for later years is attributable to the closing of the meat processing works in Ambatandrazaka, to the south in Antsihanaka. However, the unreliability of such figures is easily evident from the fact that, in reporting on numbers of cattle vaccinated for 1959, a total of 138,249 is given, which is 5,249 greater than the total number recorded in the cattle census!

Figures, apart from being inaccurate, are also misleading because one could easily get the impression that cattle were *economically* important to Tsimihety. It is recorded that in 1959 the sum of 36,532,500 Malagasy francs was earned from cattle exports from the District of Mandritsara. One would assume this was earned by Tsimihety, but, in fact, what the figures do not reveal is that most of this was earned by the 662 Antemoro, 63 Antandroy, 34 Bara, and 438 Betsileo living in Mandritsara and engaged in full-time cattle raising for commercial purposes. As well, many of the 2,055 Sihanaka, 6,431 Makoa, and 1,011 Merina bought and sold cattle. Some Tsimihety did, from time to time, sell cattle to merchants for cash, and considerably more Tsimihety rustled cattle and drove them either to the east coast or south through the forest where they sold some for cash. But these activities were for contingent and emergency purposes, or just pure acts of defiance and derring-do, as I shall discuss in a moment. Cattle, for Tsimihety, did not mean meat, or milk, or leather, or cash. In fact, cattle were less means than ends in themselves in many ways. Quality and beauty were the meaning of cattle to Tsimihety, and these characters were enhanced by the fact that cattle were limited in their utility. This made them luxuries.

Cattle were grazed on pastures (*kijany*), which were kept open and unfenced. There were good and not-so-good pastures and depending on the quality of grass and the ease of accessibility. *Adambo* and *fatakana* were tall and luscious grasses that everyone preferred. Other grasses included *kofafa, masira, hosy hosy, tsidory, apantatra, katsoaka,* and *maniviky,* which were all serviceable but less desirable. Every cattle owner in a village had equal access to pastures in the faritany, and all cattle grazed in their particular herds, but contiguously together over the land, being watched by their owner's herdsman (or boy) who took them up and brought them back. Pastures closest to the village were sometimes reserved for the cattle of the old men, as might be patches of adambo or fatakana. Neither did people crowd one another—whoever arrived first at a particular area of pasture grazed there and latecomers grazed close by.

Each village had its byre to which all cattle of the village were returned each night en masse, and though young boys and teenagers usually did the herding I have seen women and even a young girl take the cattle up. Cattle were preeminently, but not exclusively, participants in the male domain of activity. More important, wherever they were, cattle were looked after properly and with love and pleasure. Cattle care *was* a pleasure, compared to working in rice fields, which was a chore, an attitude shared by other Malagasy people (cf. Kottak 1980:156–57 for similar remarks about Betsileo).

The most important thing about cattle was not how many of them there were, but what they looked like and what their personalities were. Cattle were of the humped variety (*Bos indicus*), which often had spectacular lyre-shaped horns. They came in coats of many colors and variegated patterns and of all sizes. These were the features for which they were "valued," and the permutations of these features were the calculus of the aesthetic value of cattle.

In the brief twenty minutes or so of violet dusk, the last stragglers from the pastures were penned, and the shouting to get them into place died down. Wisps of smoke from hearth fires sneaked across the corral mingling the salty aroma of charcoal with the cloying sweetness of fresh dung and the sweaty, leathery smell of the beasts themselves. Now and again a plaintive bellow cut through the bustling sound of hooves on the ground and the rubbing of cattle against each other. In the quickly fading light everything became a monochrome. The young boys, having put their charges in the pen, saddled themselves up on the railings,

dropping their herding canes. They exchanged remarks among themselves, about the day, and especially about the antics of some particular
animal. The adult men who had returned from the fields, or who
emerged from the nearby houses, greeted each other, leaned against the
railings, and greeted the cattle, changing from a certain bland lethargic
temperament to one that soon became joyfully animated. They remarked
on the healthy appearance of their own cattle (or perhaps their thinness)
and questioned the herdboys. They admired out loud some animal that
caught their eye, boasted to neighbors of the grandeur of a favorite
beast, or, in many cases the men just leaned silently on the railings
staring with admiration at the cattle. Early on, men were only too eager
to describe for me the good points, the beautiful qualities, the fine
bearing of some animals or the weaknesses of others. Once I had learned
the form and the vocabulary, I too was able to try my hand at making
intelligent comments on the beauty of beasts, though I have to confess
less from conviction than a desire on my part to please.

Cattle were what Tsimihety talked about, the men in particular.
They were what every man was an expert about, or thought he was.
Cattle were to Tsimihety what, say, money and baseball are to Amer-
icans, or soccer and the weather to the English. Every young man had
an ambition to own the best-looking animals, or animals of a configuration that particularly appealed to him. For although there were general standards, there was also room for individual tastes and preferences.
Cattle were what Tsimihety cared about, even though they were subsistence agriculturalists, and like the Nuer of the Sudan, to understand
Tsimihety one must "cherchez la vache" (Evans-Pritchard 1940:16).
Cattle were the sine qua non for male interests, but this does not
mean to say that women were uninterested. They, too, owned animals
and admired them, but not perhaps as intensely and obsessively as
some men.

Cattle were not valued because of their subsistence or utility functions. They were rarely milked, and meat was eaten only on ritual occasions when animals were sacrificed to the ancestors. They were
occasionally used as draft animals to draw carts—leather was used to
make drum skins—but this happened hardly at all. They were used to
trample the rice fields before planting, and they were handed over as
part of the *moletry* or bridewealth payment. As I shall describe in a
moment they were often rustled, but I don't think one can say they were
valued because they were the object of rustlers' attentions. Cattle were

valued in much the same way that, in our own culture, we value collections of beautiful things—china, silver, paintings, stamps, coins, antiques, or jewelry. I think it is fair to say that every Tsimihety male expected to build up some sort of cattle collection, but some would be more successful than others. They may breed, seek desired animals in exchange, sometimes rustle. And in these tasks some people would be more diligent, more daring, more expert than others. These were the people who enjoyed prestige and a reputation and who earned respect and admiration from others less gifted or less lucky. Here, then, was a clear basis of status differential, which made some Tsimihety more equal than others. Does this contradict or undermine the political egalitarianism that I have asserted marked out Tsimihety ideology and practice? The short answer is "no," because "rank" in cattle collecting was not convertible or transferrable to any other sphere of activity or social evaluation. The situation was much like that described for many hunter/ gatherer people where hunting prowess conferred no privilege or priority in decision making.

Analysis of Cattle Aesthetics

The major attributes and qualities by which cattle were identified and described are sex, age, size, condition (including fatness and glossiness of coat), shape of horns, size of hump, color of coat, configuration of coat in terms of patches, bands, spots, and color combinations, overall configuration of the animal, and point in the life cycle.

Life-cycle points are:

betoitra	cow not yet calved
vao teraka	suckling calf
mahôta	calf just weaned
tomboay lahy/vavy	less than one year
sakantsany lahy/vavy	less than two years
vantony lahy	three-year-old bull
omby lahy/vatandreny	three-year-old heifer
katenany/vavy	four-year-old cow
doktera	ten years old or more
roka	old and toothless

These are gross categories within which the others function as refinements. These categories were identified first, before any other appraising took place, especially in any transactions for bride-price, or the selection of an animal for a sacrifice—partly because it was no good having an animal with a prize coat if it was not going to live much longer, and it was no good offering an animal to the ancestors whose meat the living will consume if it was going to be old and tough. On the other hand, it was a standing joke that one always tried to palm off to others a doktera or roka.

The horn shapes are classified as follows:

denda	extended to maximum
goroko	curled round so ends meet
dimba/dimbana	spiralled around each other
panga	pointing upward
mitsangana	lyre shaped
mivandrita/mamitsoko	long horns turning back
tsondro	turning forward
solatra	one horn turned down to muzzle
sola-droy	both horns turned down
mapoaka	one horn crooked
kôtrana	loose horns
sambilo	born with one horn
omby bory	no horns
sari-bory	stunted horns

This is roughly an order of preference, though some people would admire lyre-shaped horns (mitsangana) best of all. It was universally forbidden among all Tsimihety to offer animals without horns to ancestors or to eat the meat from such animals (they could be sold in the market, though). In one respect the horns were the most important feature of an animal because they were its most permanent distinctive feature. When a person died all visitors were given meals with meat, and the greater the number of cattle owned the larger the feasting and the more animals butchered. This proceeding limited the number of cattle inherited by heirs, and each heir essentially started from scratch. But the scale of these offerings reflected the size of the herd owned by the deceased and indicated his prestige. The only indication of the quality of the collection left after slaughter was the horns. The head and horns of each beast killed were impaled on a pole, and the collection of poles and horns or bucranes (*fisokana*) were left standing as a monument.

The coat is the most colorful and varied of the qualities of an animal. The following are the principal coat colors:

joby, mainty, maintipontry	black
tomboloho	between black and red
mena	russet to red
mavo	tan
fôtsy	white
mena maizinalina	bright red
maizinalina	very dark red
mavo alanana	fawn
marambotry	reddish fawn
kalafia	black with red
marantsifotra	russet with black

These terms were used to describe animals with plain coats. Animals with coats comprising patches of color are as follows:

Patches on the Head

mazava loha	white head, ears, base of horns
masao/msaha	white head except for ears, base of horns
marijy	blaze from base of horns
marijy sirana	uneven patches
komariko	small white patches at base of horns
bedahara	white patch in middle of face
tombo karina	slight black streak
gavo maso	white band from one eye to other
lôhan-karako	large white band between eyes
vilanorotro	patch on muzzle like harelip
lôham-panihy	like a mushroom
mavo lôha	white face, red head
makiho	white body, red ears
mena sofina	white head, red ears

(The last feature, red ears and white head, was considered the ugliest, and *sofinmena* was the term used most commonly to describe Europeans, though not usually in the hearing-range of Europeans!)

Patches on the Body

rango-tratra	scratched trunk
vakivoho	band of white on spine
volon-tety	incomplete band
babiarina	white back, black patches on rump/hump
tomangovola	white patch on top of hump
berojo	white patches on chest like necklace
dafo	patches dotted round stomach
todiaña	small patches on belly

vilazo	white patches on stomach
sampihafotra	white band round middle
fehinkira	white band on tail
vangy tety	small white patches beneath stomach
vody hangy	russet rump, neck, and head
tapa-kala	two colors dividing breast from hump
vondro-may	burnt-raphia, grayish, black nape
fangitomboka	four white feet
fotsy tanaña	rear feet white
tomany tanaña	with teardrop patches on hind legs
malandy rambo	white tail

General body patches

fitatra	spaced out patches, piebald
fita body	patches on rump
mandrovo	small gray patches, white background
tomany tanaña	as above but black background
vandaña	large color patches, dark spots
taimborana	grayish white patches (bird droppings)

The most admired of all coats were *volontsara,* the black and white coat, *vanga,* a coat with large white patches reaching down to the hooves, *haramanga,* which is the same as volontsara but uneven and not black, and *volavita,* a black and white coat with a white head and a white band from shoulder to shoulder and white haunches.

These were the main features of coats and horns specially valued, and they accord very closely with those recorded by Molet in another region occupied by Tsimihety, Ankaizina (Molet 1953).

Though any given animal was likely to present a shade or a variation that was slightly different and unique, these shadings, variations, and combinations contributed to the special mystique of a particular animal or collection. Although these were, so to speak, universal values that ranked coats, horns, and the appearance of animals, individual Tsimihety had their own preferences, and they strove to possess the animals that most appealed to them. For though a collection was for everyone's admiration, it was primarily to please its owner. The pleasure derived from the beauty of particular animals and from the harmony of a particular collection. The number of animals was a factor, but it was not the overriding factor. Numbers alone were what other Malagasy reckoned, and vazaha, especially those who raised cattle commercially. A small herd of a dozen animals that included fine specimens of volontsara, or a bull with horns denda or mitsangana, was what really counted.

Because most of a person's animals were killed for feasts upon death, and later for the exhumation and reburial (*famadihana*), everyone virtually started from scratch to build up their collection. When children were old enough to look after animals, roughly about six- to eight-years old, they were given their own animal by the father and sometimes the mother. This gift established a special bond between parent and child, and the animal represented this tie. Boys invariably received their first animal in this way, girls sometimes. Women certainly owned cattle, but they were usually merged in with the brother's herd since he looked after them. As well as being augmented by natural increase a woman's cattle collection was also added to by cattle received on marriage (moletry).

The animal a boy received from his father was always one that the father had raised from birth and on which he bestowed the earmark of his *fokondray,* of his father, which is to say of the foko in whose tomb he expected to be buried. The son, the recipient, would, under no circumstances, exchange or otherwise get rid of this animal, which was always a heifer who would provide him with calves to build up his collection. This animal, which was not, as far as I know, given any special designation, had a very high emotional value and could also be said to carry a symbolic weight.

Having received the first animal a young person set about building up a collection. Several ways were open to do this, and some were closed. No animals were bought and sold for cash, but a young man could volunteer, or comply with a request from a kinsperson, to live with and work for the household and receive at the end of this service a beast. Old people, or parents with no sons, were the ones most likely to take on such help. A young man (and sometimes a young woman) spent adolescence taking trips to various villages, mostly in search of sexual partners and prospective spouses. But among the other things they did was look for attractive animals that they might exchange for those they had raised from the original heifer. Ideally one would hope to find an animal that could augment the qualities of one's collection, or be one an individual specially wanted as an exchange for an animal the other party would particularly like. If this did not occur, then negotiations had to be entered into to exchange, for example, three two-year-old vandana with straight horns for one three-year-old tomboloho with lyre horns. There were no fixed "rates of exchange" because much depended on personal taste, on the desired composition of the herd, on the gaps in the collection, and so forth. The other major way by which young men built up their herds was rustling, which I shall describe below.

For various reasons pastures were limited for young men in particular. To counteract this people tried to disperse some of their animals into different faritany when they were building up the collection. This coincided with the need to build up a network of personal ties that would be the nucleus of one's own grapevine for finding compatible and/or exciting mates and spouses, and desirable cattle, and reliable and trustworthy contacts one could stay with on a rustling trip. Close or distant kin, and affines who lived in different parts, were obvious contacts but kin had conflicting loyalties, and so young people established the nucleus of a personal network by entering relations of blood brotherhood (*fati-dra*). The mechanics of fati-dra have their proper place elsewhere. The point of mentioning these contacts is that they were people whom one could approach to arrange for some of one's animals to be pastured out with their herds, in return for one or two calves. And equally, one could be approached by others to make similar arrangements.

Building up a collection required initiative and management, and not everyone was equally endowed with these qualities; thus, the size and composition of a collection was, to a considerable extent, indicative of the quality of a man. The attractiveness of a collection was also a reflection of an individual's taste and said much about that ineffable quality of a person—"style." A person's reputation was founded on these things.

As I have already indicated earlier, collections were depleted, too. Offerings were made to the ancestors, though usually only of one animal at a time. Many beasts were required for weddings, funerals, and fama-dihana. There was natural attrition (though people tried very hard to palm off old animals for bride-price or feasts, and those who lived near Mandritsara might try to sell old animals to the market). And there were losses from rustling. Again, these demands tested out management skills and what a man in particular possessed in cattle at any given time was an indication of his personal ability in the acquisition of "wealth" and of his taste and style. Cattle were the source of difference and inequality among people who insisted upon their political, and economic, equality.

This basic inequality became quite apparent in some cases where old men in the course of a lifetime had acquired large collections of often superior quality. The older one got the more claim one had to pasture cattle within the faritany, forcing younger men to go to the margins or to other faritany. But in large part the accumulation of a fine collection was the evolution of a man's reputation among his fellows; it was the tangible creation of the point of his secular life (as distinct from a man's passage through life to old age and becoming an ancestor). Yet, however large and fine the collection, hence however glowing a man's reputation as reflected in his cattle career, it never put him in a distinct and superior category or class that excluded others from social, political, or any sort of intercourse. Nor did it bestow any political or social privilege. Nor was it a reputation that extended beyond the bounds of the individual to his kin. Only when it came to cattle talk was the successful individual deferred to or looked upon with a degree of respect. There were very few "heroes" of this ilk. The only hero I met was reported to own several hundred cattle, including some prize specimens. He was also a "character," an eccentric. He had built a large house of traditional mud and dung, but of his own design, a quasi-European two-storied affair but with edges and windows rounded. He himself was tall, upright, wore a dark blue military (naval?) greatcoat with silver buttons and always carried a silver-topped cane. (In this he echoed the "uniform" of Sakalava mpanjaka.) His goatee beard and silver hair topped off a splendid aristocratic impression. Within his village, and tanindrazana, he was a man greatly respected and closely listened to at meetings of the rayamandreny, but beyond those boundaries he had no influence at all. Only his reputation went beyond these boundaries into Androna. What was interesting to me was that I often heard him compared favorably with President Tsiranana because he came near to being the ideal Tsimihety—independent, rich in cattle, loyal to kin, and a respecter of fomba Tsimihety. President Tsiranana, on the other hand, had gone from Androna to Antananarivo, and had become mpanjaka and a paid member of the government, in short a vazaha or foreigner.

Owning cattle was not a privilege. All men, and many women, expected, as a right, to own cattle and to make it possible for others to do so. Children owned cattle. This universal right, understood as a matter of course, was a fundamental expression of Tsimihety equality. This factor was asserted even more strongly by virtue of the fact that the subsistence value of cattle was near zero. This means, translated into our own economic terms, that all were equal in rights to wealth, to the things that mattered but which were not matters of necessity. Hence they

The village of Ankiabe Salohy

Five brothers—elders of their village

Boxing (*morengy*)—the first to hit wins

Weaving raphia cloth

A young husband and wife combine to plant rice.

Cattle trampling rice to extract the grain (*magnosy*)

Wrestling an ox prior to butchering

Exhausted, the ox is to be offered to the ancestors.
The bride's father sprinkles it first with water.

Investing the bride with her wardrobe (*misarona*)

The groom's father and father's brother address the bride's people.

Men and women pound rice together for a funeral meal.

The elders maintaining vigil and being offered meat. The corpse lies behind the curtains.

A rock tomb—note the jackets, cane, coins, plate, glass, and cup. The tomb will be sealed.

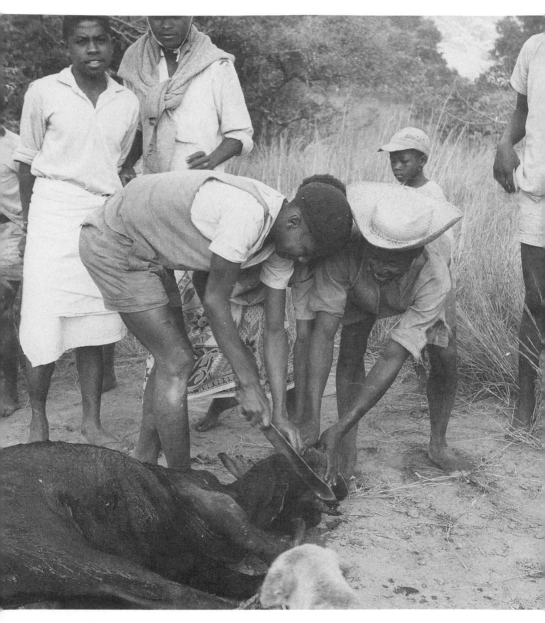

The sacrificial cut is made quite nonchalantly.

Mpijoro offering a prayer to the ancestors

were expressions of freedom in an almost Kantian sense. Because Tsimihety did not depend on cattle for subsistence, it can be said they had chosen (or willed) that what mattered universally to them, gave a special meaning to their lives as Tsimihety, was the raising and collection of cattle. That some people were distinctly better and more successful did not, in fact, matter—for it did not make them any more free, any more Tsimihety. They simply underlined for everyone else what really mattered. Hence they were not envied and neither were they privileged. Their pleasure at their hundreds of fine cattle was not different in kind from the pleasure of the average individual at his collection of five or ten.

I therefore do not agree with Molet's (1953) conclusion that cattle were important to Tsimihety because they were functional, especially because they had an important function in ritual. My argument is quite the opposite, that cattle were important precisely because they were *not* functional. I do not deny that cattle served functions. They were sacrificed or offered to ancestors in all cases where ancestors had to be firmly persuaded to either help the living or to desist from interfering. Ancestors and the living had to be fed meat on such occasions as weddings, funerals, and exhumations. And sometimes cattle were offered in gratitude for recovery, for a successful outcome, as in the fulfillment of a conditional promise. But offerings and sacrifices could be made of things other than cattle, such as chickens, goats, and alcohol. Cattle were kept for the big events, as the final resort; the reason this might have been so, I suggest, was because they were the most precious and beautiful things Tsimihety had to offer. Cattle were not prized and beautiful *because* they were used in rituals; they were used in rituals because they were beautiful. And because they were also the objectification and symbol of Tsimihety freedom and equality the sacrifice of cattle was the sacrifice of the ultimate—freedom and equality. Rituals are dependency, but a freely chosen dependency. The marginality of cattle to functional and economic value put Tsimihety outside (though not beyond) ensnarement in the cash economy of colonialism and, latterly, central government and a national economy. The encroachments of administration on cattle, through demands that they be registered and a license obtained everytime they were to be moved, was a source of great irritation to Tsimihety and one that they had no compunction about evading, because they sensed it was the thin end of the wedge that would lead them into dependency and subservience.

Cattle and Cohesion

It seems to me that the love Tsimihety bore toward their cattle as the means through which they could express their aesthetic aspirations and propensities sets Tsimihety apart from other Malagasy and especially from Europeans. In their own eyes, and contrary to an observer's perception of what was the case, Tsimihety considered themselves pastoralists. All Malagasy attach great importance to cattle, but as far as Tsimihety were concerned, they were the only ones who treated cattle as important for their own sake and not as a source of food or income. There are a sufficient number of remarks and offhand observations in my notes that suggest this may well be the way Tsimihety regarded their own attitude toward cattle and toward other Malagasy. In passing, people made disparaging observations and remarks about the Bara who lived among them to raise cattle commercially, and a number of men observed to me, and among themselves, that the Merina who lived in Androna did not have the slightest ability to raise decent cattle and did not seem to care about cattle.

Cattle concentrated the attention of Tsimihety, and this sharing of attention was undoubtedly a factor that contributed to their sense of belonging together as people of a common set. There was another, far more active pursuit that focused on cattle and which could be understood both as an expression of their consuming interest and as a means of real binding through commitment. This activity was rustling.

In the years immediately before my arrival the meat works at Ambatondrazaka was in full operation, and I was told that many of the animals received there were stolen by "professional" cattle thieves. Some of these may well have been Tsimihety, and at least three men confessed to me, not without a tinge of pride, that they had successfully engaged in stealing and selling. But by 1962 the meat works was being phased out of operation and was not buying cattle. This did not, however, put a stop to rustling in Androna although the numbers of cattle stolen did drop. But the frequency of raids was still high.

For a while men were cagey about rustling. I obtained an idea of its scale from attending a court hearing in Mandritsara, and then I was present in a village when it was the victim of a raid. In any case, spending just a short time in a village one could not help but overhear men talking among themselves about cattle and stealing. After a while I found men quite ready to talk about it as something of which they were proud. The pride was attached both to the activity and to the fact that it stated a defiance of government (the full penalty for rustling was 20 years' imprisonment).

A man never undertook to steal on his own but always as a member of a small band of between three and six men. Sometimes a gang would come from the same village, but more commonly it would comprise young men from different, but neighboring, villages. Commonly the initiator and leader was an older man, often a man driven by a desire to own a particular animal he had seen on his travels, or which had been reported to him. But young men, who traveled around the area a lot, as often as not made a note of desirable animals, or pasturing conditions in a village that made animals particularly vulnerable. Not all expeditions were successful, though. The one time I was included we set off on a pitch-black night and, after walking for hours without arriving in sound of any cattle, decided to sleep out the rest of the night. When we awoke we found we had walked in circles and were no more than a hundred or so meters from our own village!

Rustling was a daring, risky business. A successful mission was an experience that first required that members of a band had a good basis for trusting one another, and then it provided them with a bonding that came from sharing in danger. Through participation in rustling young men had a chance to create overlapping circles of special friendships that continued throughout their lives and which spanned not just years but distant domiciles. But women were not entirely excluded from all this. Not only must the gang trust each other, they also needed to establish a range of contacts who would provide them, and their stolen cattle, with hospitality as they drove them to their destinations. Women were often among these contacts. And the principal way in which trusty contacts were ensured was through blood brotherhood (*fati-dra*).

Fati-dra was a reciprocal relationship in which both parties undertook to assist each other when such assistance was needed. It was a properly quasi-kinship relationship in that fati-dra should not marry and neither should their children. It was entered into privately but with due solemnity and ritual, each party drawing blood from the chest, dipping rice grains in it, and then swallowing the grains. But no officiant was required. I was told that blood brotherhood was on the wane. Nevertheless I spoke to seventeen men from five villages who were engaged in cattle rustling and who all had fati-dra. Eleven of these men were younger than thirty years and eight of these were married. One man said he went on his first raid when he was ten years old and he made his first fati-dra. These younger men all had fati-dra but were not willing to tell me how many they had or to identify them, which was fair enough given the circumstances. The other six men were all elderly. One admitted to having five blood brothers, three to having eight, and two to having nine. Their fati-dra included women as well as men. Some of the blood brothers had died, but ties and contacts with the living were still kept up. It was my impression that fati-dra mapped out both the composition of rustling gangs and lines of contact and hospitality extending through Androna. Fati-dra were personal networks of special friends superimposed on the networks of kin along which an individual traced his movements, sought his companions, and garnered his information. In this sense, then, Tsimihety were drawn together, though not as an organized political group. Since cattle rustling was against the law and the law was enforced by the government, engaging in it was an act of defiance of the government and gained from this a particular piquancy. To rustle was to express Tsimihety independence and this brought forth a solidarity among all Tsimihety, even though they were the victims. But they dealt with rustling in their own way.

Rarely would rustlers actually be caught. Usually they had managed to disperse the stolen animals into prearranged pastures and villages before any search party could get together. But the same lines of kin who provided a safety net of hospitality for rustlers were also an intelligence service for the victims of a raid. A stolen beast might be spotted and word sent around. There were certainly occasions when people who had been robbed had a very good idea of who the thieves were. On at least one occasion witnessed by me, the fokon'olona of the villages involved (victims and violators) came together—with the one making accusations and the other defending its members. But for the most part a victim waited for information or sought it out; then, rather than engaging in open confrontation and accusation, either prepared a raid to get back his animals and then some more, or planned a raid to steal cattle from the thief's herd. Rustling therefore took on the form of a potential feud in which sets of people engaged with each other in a mutually daring manner as two teams in a sport. And it was a sport rather than a deadly earnest enterprise of life and death, with which the notion of the feud is normally associated. But there was no association between these reciprocating "games," and such Tsimihety groupings as villages, zafintany, or more generally the foko. Rustling and counter-rustling were individual pursuits. A raid was initiated by an individual, who recruited his assistants. A protest was initiated by an individual, who mobilized his resources. Because of its ongoing, tit-for-tat nature, rustling did not upset the equilibrium of social relations other than in a purely temporary fashion.

Gender and Seniority

The formal kinship terminology (see Wilson 1967) was marked by distinctions based on generation, relative age, and gender. In as much as kinship terms and their distinctions were taken for granted by the people who used them, these distinctions were also features of people's behavior and general attitudes to one another. People who were kin were distinguished from one another by virtue of seniority—senior generations always had precedence over junior generations. Within generations, as with siblings for example, the elder sibling had precedence over the younger sibling. Precedence in this case meant formal seniority, as when the spokesperson (soja) or ritual officiant (mpijoro) was automatically the senior male of the senior generation in the relevant context, all other things being equal (being of sound mind, for example). The senior sibling was publicly responsible, in the first instance, for looking after the interests of younger siblings, as when the elder brother was the first choice of a woman as the guardian of her cattle when she left her village after marriage. The responsibilities and authority of the eldest brother increased considerably on the death of the father, and it was he who acted on their behalf both ritually (as mpijoro) and secularly.

The difference between male and female indicated in the terminology became hierarchical in actual behavior. In family circumstances the final authority over a household, or over an extended family or a dispersed sibling group, rested with the senior male. In everyday life, as seen in public, male precedence over female was evident: females always walked behind males (and younger children always followed older children); the woman served food to the man and his guests in the hut (not the kitchen) in a servile kneeling position, tasting the food first; in public women tended to carry the burden while men walked relatively unencumbered; in public women deferred to men when speaking (though at kabary women had their say, especially if the matter concerned them or their close kin). It was certainly the case, then, that women appeared to be subordinate to men, and that younger was subordinate to older. There was an inequality among Tsimihety. However, inequality of the sexes was not as rigid and hierarchical as first appeared. On an ordinary day, when there were no visitors from afar, men and women often ate together in the kitchen, around the fire. Individuals helped themselves, or one might ask another to hand over a corncob, or to refill a bowl with rice. Older women in particular tended to spend long periods sitting by the fire talking and keeping an eye on the cooking pots and on the young children who clustered around. Men often came and went from the kitchen. Young children in the care of the elder sisters mixed in with grandparents around the fire where they snacked (often on insects) and played. In the evenings, for a short while before going to sleep, members of a household relaxed together in the pleasure of each others' company, male and female, elder and junior.

Unmarried adolescent girls of a village often did things together as a group: they looked after young children, they searched out wild fruits, they swam in the river. Young men, if they were not working, cruised around together, and from time to time organized intervillage boxing matches (*maraingy*), or hunted together in the forest for lemur and fruit bats. The sexes of all ages used separate areas in the bush for latrines. As I have already noted, unmarried men and women of a village received partners in their own designated quarters.

Apart from the specific tasks performed by the two sexes in rice cultivation, there was a generally accepted division of labor between the sexes. Women washed clothes (usually in the river), pounded rice each morning for the day's meals, and supervised the granary. Women swept out the sleeping hut each morning, hanging up the sleeping mats on the wall. Men and women collected firewood, but women more generally took responsibility for maintaining the fire and for the cooking on an everyday basis. Men, however, cooked when large numbers of people had to be entertained, and this included preparing the food, doing such otherwise female tasks as rice pounding. Tsimihety were not industrious craftspeople, producing artifacts and items only as needed and, with the exception of metalware, all items were produced for oneself. Women wove raphia cloth on small, back looms (not all women wove, and weaving was entirely a matter of individual choice). Women made baskets for household use and hats for men were woven as well. Eating mats, always finely woven and small in size, and larger sleeping mats were also woven by women. Men made furniture from raphia palm wood, and built houses and ox carts. Some men were skilled in making the Tsimihety drum (*amponga*), and the Tsimihety variant of the Malagasy national instrument, the valiha. Tsimihety valiha were made by splitting a raphia branch, halving it, hollowing it out, binding the two halves together, and gouging out the strings from the bark. Very few men made instruments, and the imported accordion was far more common. In Androna there were about half a dozen blacksmiths, men who fashioned blades for knives and slashers and sickles. The steel was from used car-leaf springs, which Tsimihety obtained either directly from merchants in Majunga or from local Indian merchants in Mandritsara. Each ironsmith had a couple of assistants working the piston bellows and handing things to him. Ironworkers were not full-time specialists, and they only worked (1) after the rice harvest and (2) when enough people had ordered. Payment was in rice, cattle, or sometimes cash. In some areas of Androna, particularly to the west near the banks of the Sofia River, sugarcane was grown. The sugar, in large cakes, was bartered throughout the region and was also used to make rum. The fermented juice (betsabetsa) was made by every household, but the distilled spirit (taoka), which was widely used for ritual purposes, was made only by a few specialists, all of them men. Although salt could be obtained from merchants in Mandritsara, and from the small shops operated by Merina in one or two of the larger villages, most Tsimihety obtained salt by barter trade with Betsimisaraka, who visited Tsimihety villages on a regular basis carrying tubes of salt that they had made by slowly burning the inner bark of a tree into an ash and packing it in leafy tubes. This salt, and honey, was traded with Tsimihety for rice. Since the rice granaries and the rice supply were managed by women, it was women who were engaged in this trade.

There were social distinctions premised on gender among Tsimihety, and these distinctions were formally hierarchical. In public etiquette, women were treated, and acted, as subordinates to men, just as younger people acted subordinately to older people. This formal gender and age hierarchy also provided a general blueprint for basic social intercourse both in the intimacy of the household and more publicly in the village. However, Tsimihety were not formal people. The smallness of their hamlets and villages, for example, made a distinction between the private domestic realm and the public domain very hazy, and the requirements of easy interaction prevailed over restraints of classification and status. Public behavior was defined as behavior that took place at certain times rather than in certain places: times of death, times of dispute, times of marriage, times of welcome to visitors, all of which occurred in the same space as ordinary everyday behavior. If visitors were present, for example, especially if those visitors were strangers, then the formality with which those visitors were treated required that Tsimihety observe the formalities of age and gender hierarchy. It was a long time before I was able to appreciate this, since my very presence made the occasion a formal one.

The formal rules of deference and demeanor based on relative age and sex were always subjected to circumstances and to personality. Here is one example when all the formal rules were broken. Lehova was over seventy years old and had recently been married to a girl of nineteen. Everyone thought that this simply confirmed that he was a "character." Much to his delight and pride his wife became pregnant. He decided the child should be born in the hospital, as this was the modern and advanced (vazaha) thing to do. Before dawn the two of them set off to walk the twenty-five kilometers to Mandritsara. I met them, by accident, about fifteen kilometers out when I was driving to a particular village. He was walking by her side, one arm steadying her and the other carrying their bundle of supplies. He flagged me down, ordered me to take them to the hospital, and then, in the back of the Landrover he attended to his young wife with gentle solicitousness. Later, after their return home, he waited on her and the baby as well as doted on them. Age and gender did not come into it.

Conclusion

One thing I found especially difficult to come to grips with when living among Tsimihety, and later when trying to write about them, was their apparently atrophied aesthetic life. How could people who were part and parcel of a countrywide culture rich in funeral art, secular music, oratory and poetry, and decoration be so uninterested in both the idea and the practice of an aesthetic?

Of course, one can always say that this absence of aesthetic was part of what made up Tsimihety as opposed to any other Malagasy. But that does not get one very far. Significantly, Tsimihety indulged in one form of decoration consistently: women took great trouble over their hairstyle. Two women would dress each other's hair in a selected style about once a week, using oil and animal fat. Four styles were favoured: *antimivono,* a style with numerous plaits sticking out; *randranamandiniky,* little plaits tied in patterns over the head; *taly koja,* where the hair was plaited to form a chain effect; and *bada bada,* the most favored style, worn by a bride, for example, where the hair was plaited and then formed into two "balls" placed like earphones over the ears. Such decoration was decoration without distinction in that so long as a woman had hair she could "make up" and appear as beautiful as the next person. Hairstyles did not distinguish the beautiful from the ugly person. Nor were hairstyles individual possessions that could be used to measure anything, and they did not have to be paid for, as did cloth for clothes. (If Tsimihety women wore western-style dresses instead of sarongs [*salovana*] they wore all that they possessed at the same time and discarded them over the years. These dresses were often acquired at marriage, and once they were worn out women wore the sarong).

My proposed answer to the problem of the "meaning" of an atrophied aesthetic expression is part of my more general reconstitution of the jigsaw that made up Tsimihety freedom and equality, their constitution as a "set." I have already identified aesthetic atrophy as part of a process of "cultural flattening," but in this chapter I have been suggesting that aesthetics has, for the most part, been diverted and concentrated into cattle. Cattle were the wealth of the agricultural Tsimihety as distinct from the property they held in land. But possession of wealth was the open road to inequality, so how can this be reconciled with Tsimihety egalitarianism and the freedom that is braided in and out?

Cattle could not be converted or used as part of a cash or exchange economy. They were severed in all but a few minor instances from the subsistence economy so that, as wealth, they could not contribute to the transformation of that subsistence economy to a surplus economy. Cattle were not bought and sold among Tsimihety, and were only sold to outsiders in an emergency, or by those living close to markets, where there was a certain amount of pressure put on them by consumers (government employees mostly), though they were exchanged for labor and at marriage. Cattle were not inherited in any number, so there was only individually acquired wealth. Cattle, then, can only be measured against each other and, in this sense, were the center of a closed system of values. Even when used in ritual offerings to ancestors they remained within the closed system, for the ancestors were continuous with the living, and beasts offered to them were offered for their aesthetic qualities. When visitors came for weddings and funerals, the obligation to feed them meat did not impose an obligation to impress them with more than they could eat. It was far more important that hosts kept face by offering distinguished beasts and that they came up to expectations, not that they put on a great display in a feast of such proportions that meat might be left over. Of course there were subtleties involved, as when people might turn up knowing the meat resources were great and push hosts beyond what they might have been expecting to provide. This also served to bring cattle owned back to something like a parity with everyone else. But a man who owned many cattle garnered no political prestige; he could not "buy" followers, or even assistants, sidekicks, and yes-men.

Tsimihety aesthetic life, almost as much for women as for men, was concentrated in the appreciation of the fine points of cattle. Tsimihety were a sort of "cattle club"; they were like the horsey crowd of English or American society who were drawn together by their enthusiasm and love of horses. A beautiful animal was a joy for all to behold, and although the owner enjoyed a special feeling of pride from such appreciation and praise the owner got no power, no sense that he or she was a better person. It is the love of beauty embodied in animals that makes both horsey Englishmen and "boviney" Tsimihety equally one of a kind. And yet, for Tsimihety, the mechanics of building a collection allowed each and every individual scope for self-expression, for achieving self-esteem and a reputation among others. And that is what Tsimihety did, what made people all equal as Tsimihety, superior to and different from such other Malagasy as Merina, Bara, Betsileo, Sakalava, Betsimisaraka, and the rest.

The aesthetic of cattle as well as the absolutely central part they played in the imaginative life of Tsimihety is further evidenced in the fact that the only toys Tsimihety children had were model cattle made of sun-dried mud. These models portrayed animals with huge horns and humps, identifying the appealing properties and, perhaps, reflecting the more general cultural ideal. Small boys and girls built miniature corrals of twigs and moved the models in and out. Occasionally the model animals were hitched to a model cart.

Cattle were also looked upon with a certain awe and reverence as well as aesthetic appreciation. I presume this derived from their role in offerings (*joro*) to both ancestors and spirits (*zanahary*). Cattle placated both spirits and ancestors as well as rewarded them and acted as intermediaries between the living and the supernatural. Cattle were the principal way in which the living could influence the supernatural. This brought forth the respect of the living for cattle and was the source of their sense of duty to treat animals well. When the living and the supernatural have entered into a contract and the supernatural powers have delivered, the living kept their part of the bargain by offering cattle. Cattle then were the primary currency units for important transactions between the living and the supernatural. In this sense cattle had ritual importance in a sort of ritual economy. This also helps us to understand the exclusiveness, the closed system that embraced cattle and Tsimihety. Cattle mediated between the living, the ancestors, and the spirits, and that was all. No outsiders, not even other Malagasy, could have a place in these transactions. And these transactions defined the one hierarchy that Tsimihety considered politically valid, the hierarchy which grouped together all the living versus the group of all the supernatural, especially the ancestors. Cattle were the link between the two echelons.

In gender and relative age there were formal distinctions of precedence and dominance that were crystallized in the kinship terminology and in the visible, public behavior of people in meetings, rituals, and the like. Much of this differentiation, I am inclined to suggest, existed as a property of the Malagasy wide culture that Tsimihety inherited with the language, but which was either anachronistic or inappropriate in their own egalitarian way of life. An indication of the balance between male and female was more evident in Tsimihety marriage, an institution that Tsimihety continued to mold to their own purposes far more consciously and easily than they could change the classificatory systems of Malagasy language and culture. I shall describe marriage later in the next chapter.

Appendix

All Tsimihety cattle, like cattle belonging to all other Malagasy groups, were identified by distinctive earmarks. Each design was associated with a named ancestral grouping (foko). A man's first heifer was always marked with the design of his father, hence his father's foko. But with exchanges, rustling, and the like, a person's collection contained animals with a mixture of marks. So actual ownership marks for personal identification were made by branding. In this Tsimihety differ from the interpretation put forward by Birkeli in his authoritative study of Malagasy earmarks (1926). Birkeli maintains these earmarks indicate private property, but since the earmarks are ancestral and are badges of the foko they cannot indicate private individual property anyway. And as cattle among Tsimihety were never owned collectively, the marks did not indicate collective private property. Figure 1 depicts the most frequently occurring earmarks among Tsimihety of Androna. They tally closely, but are not identical with those given by Birkeli.

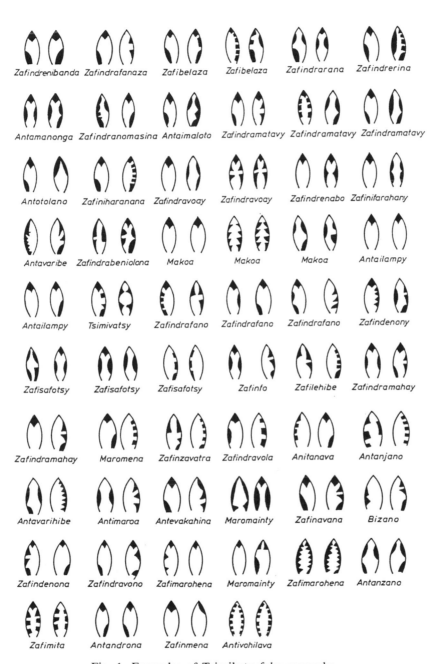

Fig. 1. Examples of Tsimihety *foko* earmarks

CHAPTER 4

Fraternité

I have argued earlier that the value of any statistics about Tsimihety is virtually nil. But suppose for a moment we were to accept the population estimate for the early 1900s, which was 35,000, and for about 1950, which was roughly 363,000. In fifty years there has been a tenfold increase, which receives no mention from the commentators citing these statistics. Yet this is a staggering increase—especially since it does not appear Tsimihety were more fertile than other Malagasy, that their mortality rates were that much lower, or that they were better served by modern medical services. Valueless as the statistics may be as an accurate measure, I think it reasonable to assume they were compiled to reflect a real situation, namely that Tsimihety had certainly expanded demographically. I think this expansion was by way of immigration as well as by natural increase. People had moved into Androna, and as they settled they regarded themselves, and were regarded by others, as Tsimihety. However, as far as I could tell from census figures, surrounding populations of Betsimisaraka, Sihanaka, and Sakalava did not show a corresponding decrease. On the other hand, authorities such as Deschamps and Molet had noted a geographical expansion of Tsimihety westward and northward, though neither related this to demographic expansion. It seems to me, though, that all these evidences and queries suggest that the demographic expansion of Tsimihety may be explained in part by natural increase, in part by immigration, and partially by absorption of local people in the areas to which Tsimihety had migrated. Taking these factors into consideration, as well as the mobility of Tsimihety within Androna, and the other traditional Tsimihety regions, it seems fair to say that for all their desire to distance themselves from the outside, and outsiders, this distancing was selective. For, in another sense, Tsimihety were open, flexible, and accommodating, and they lacked a sense of being special or of being focused and reined in by ritualized political institutions, such as those centering on the Sakalava mpanjaka or the Merina Palace and its former monarchs.

So how was a sense of being Tsimihety achieved or maintained in face of this remarkable, almost anarchically open way of life? Or to phrase the question at another level: How did the individual achieve a sense of security and stability under such conditions of freedom and mobility? I have already discussed how, without security of tenure in land, the individual Tsimihety had security of usufruct, and hence there was subsistence security. In the previous chapter I discussed the sense in which Tsimihety achieved security in wealth by investing reputation and artistic expression in cattle. Cattle, being movable, were no hindrance to mobility, and the natural increase in cattle was countered as a means of individual inequality by the virtual destruction of wealth at death. But what of the emotional security and well-being that comes from a security of social life? Was such a security possible under the conditions of demographic and geographic mobility and expansion? Was it possible under the conditions of political evasion of external authority and political egalitarianism? Was the ideal of political liberty extended to individual social liberty? Where was the limit to such freedoms situated among Tsimihety?

Traditionally in social anthropology the concept of a social structure has been presented as an autonomous constraining social fact. Recent ethnography has reacted against this idea, because it assumes an unjustifiable authorial authority and ignores the social construction of social facts, especially kinship and descent.

Kinship is important in my own life and that of my wife, though descent is not. But in twentieth-century urban New Zealand, descent and descent groups are of increasingly prominent social and political importance for both European and Maori people. I am therefore not about to deny kinship and descent their importance, let alone their existence. Though exactly what their ontological status is I shall leave unexamined. So, from purely subjective premises as well as from the clear insistence in my fieldnotes and memory upon terms, ideas, and practices that corresponded to my own, and to general anthropological ideas of kinship and descent, I want to try to describe the regular principles that appear to have guided individuals to find security and stability from each other but which did not constrain them, at least to the extent that social and political life became incompatible with liberty and mobility. And, if Tsimihety were as open as their rapid increase in population suggests, then the individual's security and enjoyment of well-being with others could not be as exclusive as the many accounts of social structure suggest, even among other Malagasy peoples such as the tomb groups described by Bloch for the Merina.

Mobility

Tsimihety were mobile people. Urban western people are mobile as well. One difference between the mobility of my own life, for example, and that of Tsimihety is that I have moved to places where I knew no one. I moved from one institution (a university or college) to another in different parts of the world. It could easily have been a company rather than a university. I made friends in each place, and in one place acquired in-laws as well. These friendships and affines are now selective destinations for many of my travels, but if I move to live and work elsewhere it will still be because of an institutional attraction, not a social one. As I grow older I feel a sense of loss, of missing out, of distance from something I vaguely call my own tradition, or from the cultural history I grew up in and had the ambition to contribute toward. But fundamentally my social existence is immediate, local, and without deep commitment.

Tsimihety often had materialistic motives for moving; they frequently moved in search of access to better pastures and, less often, to better rice fields. But such a search was never independent of kin. Individuals trekked along invisible lines of kinship to villages where pastures might be greener, or more accessible. Tsimihety moved for other reasons of a more social, or even ritual, nature. Living in a village meant living intimately with neighbors, and for many people there was a limit to the length of time when one's kin or fellow villages were also good neighbors. People moved following their own personal likes and dislikes of other people. Living in a particular village may have coincided with an unfortunate period of life—illness, bad luck, bad dreams, quarrels, premonitions. Following the advice of consultants who worked by divination (*mpisikidy*) people would move. But a move was never blind; it was always to another place where one was known to at least some of the inhabitants. For one thing, no villagers would accept a complete stranger to live in their midst—which was an important reason why I found it so difficult to live in a village. But just being known was not usually enough; there had to be a deeper identification between the villager and the intending settler, an identification that could lead to trust, to the removal of any fears. The only sound basis for this was kinship between an inhabitant and a settler, as if the integrity and good intentions of the settler could be "read off" from knowledge of the inhabitant through the tie, or rather metaphor, of kinship.

Kinship in relation to mobility was enabling rather than restrictive, for since kinship was divorced from ownership but tied to usufruct it did not exercise a restraining or excluding function. Anyone moving *into* a village could seek the right to use land to live on, cultivate, and graze without threatening to control these resources. If the relationship was based on zafintany status, the incoming individual was granted use of land as a right; if the immigrant status was less direct (vahiny), rights to use land were granted conditionally and temporarily, theoretically on a year-to-year basis. These same kinship ties imposed few constraints on the individuals wishing to move *out* of a village since emigration did not mean forfeit of title. The land was "owned" by the ancestors in the tomb and those among the living who would ascend to ancestorship by occupying a place in the tomb. So, wherever Tsimihety went, they could not abandon the tanindrazana, though the bonds did become more and more attenuated.

Having said that kinship enabled migration because kin were the initial range of choices from which to select probable destinations, I have to note the exceptions to this generalization. The first is those Tsimihety who homesteaded. I have no idea of the proportion of Tsimihety who might have homesteaded during the course of their lives. In Androna, during my travels I came across six homesteads. Two included a man, his wife, and adolescent and young children. The other four were older and younger brothers and their respective families. These were people who set about clearing dense bush land, which they said had never been settled (i.e., virgin bush). If successful, they would attract their kin and eventually carve out a faritany that, when a tomb was opened, would become a tanindrazana. Their migration and settlement had been independent of kinship ties. The other exception concerned Tsimihety who emigrated to Tananarive or Majunga to secure an education and/or a bureaucratic or political occupation. I can say little of such people as I only met those who happened to return to Androna while I was there. They were all men who had lived in lodgings to begin with, though I would imagine Tsimihety sought out Tsimihety in the big cities.

Tsimihety migration was not, in any way, predatory or colonial. Tsimihety migrated as individuals or small kinship groups as a result of their individual decisions. There was simply no organization that inspired or directed a Tsimihety expansion. Even when it was decided that a particular village was too spiritually contaminated to live in, its inhabitants did not necessarily move en bloc. They may have chosen to do so, but, equally, separate households may have chosen to go their own way. Molet has tried to outline a pattern of Tsimihety migration: the first generation clears the land, the second generation consolidates and settles, and the third generation moves out and on, leaving some behind to maintain continuity (Molet 1959:112). As long as this is not considered a deliberate plan that Tsimihety follow, but a general pattern which roughly emerged, I think Molet's model is a good summary. But it was punctuated by people migrating for personal reasons (dislike of neighbors, wanderlust, desire for adventure, or change of scenery) as well as for more rational motives subject to generalization. Tsimihety, I am suggesting, were free to choose when and where to move, and their moves were not determined by any sort of independent social structure, by social facts sui generis, or, for that matter, by ecological pressures. In addition, under conditions first of Merina, then of French domination, moving around to avoid detection and domination emerged as a successful political tactic. This, and retreat to the hills or the forest, was a tactic that was continued after independence as a means of avoiding government officials, missionaries, and anthropologists.

Distinct from moving from one residence to another was the practice of visiting (*mamangy*). There were formal, or more accurately perhaps, expected visits between people, and informal or unexpected aspects of visiting. Yet so pervasive was the fondness for visiting by both men and women, but especially by women, that I am tempted to say visiting was a customary aspect of Tsimihety life. Especially in the dry season a village invariably hosted several visitors. My own forced pattern of visiting rather than staying in villages was approved, but I would often arrive to continue an interview or renew an acquaintance only to find my contact was away visiting.

As I have already mentioned each village set aside an empty house for visitors, or vacated one if there was not one standing empty. Young people entertained partners of the opposite sex in their own huts (kotralahy/kotravavy). These casual visitors were fed as well as housed but were not expected to stay long, perhaps one or two nights. Any longer and they became objects of suspicion—villagers felt they were being spied on. And indeed they often were, since visitors kept their eyes open for likely spouses, likely cattle, good rice fields, and vacant pastures.

More formal visiting was associated with marriage. Fifteen days after a wedding the husband and wife returned to her village bearing small gifts (*fotitra andro*). This visit was intended to show that the woman was happy, that it had been a good match, and it was the beginning of the effort a man made to get on good terms with his in-laws. It was frequently the case that there were better opportunities in the wife's village, or that her elderly or ailing parents needed help. In such cases a newly married couple might settle down in her village first and the husband render his in-laws services. In return for such services, on the grounds that he had been instrumental in keeping land in cultivation, the husband, through his wife, might come to enjoy more permanent rights of usufruct. When a man lived in his wife's village he frequently made visits back to his parents' village. Three months after a marriage a woman returned to her village alone and thereafter returned every year with young children and infants in tow. If possible a woman timed her visit to coincide with that of her sisters so there was an annual family reunion. In between, sisters made a habit of visiting each other, which was probably important psychologically because a wife had to face in-laws and, unless she happened to hit it off with them or with the other married women who had come into the village, she would have no one to turn to for intimacy and sympathy. Once back in her village a woman and her children visited the households of her kinfolk living there and in the villages of the faritany, a pattern called *mitsidika*. The overall effect of all this visiting was that it kept active and vivid kinship ties that might have faded because of geographical distance. In fact a woman (or man) who was a diligent visitor was highly praised and comple-mented—"*zay mamangy vangy tiankavana.*"

Tsimihety, then, were people on the move. Their horizons were not limited to the village and the surrounding fields. Nor were their social lives hemmed in. Given the penchant for visiting, and the fact that settlement in any given place was never thought of as permanent, any individual knew many others all over Androna as well as his or her immediate neighbors. Tsimihety were neither local nor parochial. As I shall discuss later, the more formal institutions of marriage, in particular, were based on, at the same time as they furthered, this sense of mobility and expansion.

For all this freedom of movement the individual need never be unattached or thrown so much upon his own devices and chance that the immense freedom he enjoyed left him insecure. Stated another way, the range of choice of where to go, or who to look to, was not infinite or formless; it was shaped and delimited, as I have indicated, by kinship. If I were to attempt a functional explanation of kinship among Tsimihety I would argue for its role in contributing to the drawing of the line between Tsimihety and other Malagasy and for its function as setting out the contours of Androna as a social landscape. Kinship meant people knew where to go and how to get there. As kinship clarified into ascent it became two-dimensional, guiding the individual not only through space but also through time. And ascent embodied in the tomb was like the diver's lifeline and support system that allowed freedom of movement with the assurance of a safe return.

Kinship

As a terminological system Tsimihety kinship can be analyzed in quite formal terms (cf. Wilson 1967). It specified the fine grading of relationship and the nuancing of people's respect for each other taken separately from their regard and affection. But it would, I think, be a mistake to rely on the formal properties of kinship terminology to convey the "meaning" of kinship. If anything kinship was the key to Tsimihety informality, and informality was more characteristic of their social lives than formality. This was what one might expect from people who had discarded rank as a dimension of social and political life. The point about having kin, and being with kin, was that these were people with whom one could relax and let down one's guard. With strangers and nonkin you had to watch out all the time—you had to beware of motives and intentions, and you just didn't know what strangers were like or how to deal with them. (Suspicion of strangers was greatly aggravated by the infiltration of political PSD agents and informers.) People who were not kin were dangerous, and this distinction is one that is emphasized by Bloch in his description of Merina kinship (1971:58–61). But I am not at all sure that morality is the main significance of *havana* (kinship), as Bloch argues. People who are havana to each other are not, by that definition, good or bad. People who are havana can notoriously arouse passionate reactions in each other by taking advantage, by pressing demands beyond the limit and so forth. Nonkin, such as vahiny with whom one has lived in some intimacy, can be good people who can be trusted. Havana are people one can most likely trust (or mistrust) not because they are by definition trustworthy but because one either knows them directly, or indirectly, in that they may be understood to be like the people one knows as kin. This is not the same as assuming that havana are "good."

Havana was the general term for kinship of any form, as it was throughout Madagascar. In one sense it was the outermost protective social layer for the individual. It included any and all persons to whom an individual could trace a real, or an imagined, kinship link. It was a personal, or ego-centered, network or umbrella involving relatives through both parents and including affines. I doubt whether any individual could specify all his or her havana, so it was not really a concept useful for social or individual definition. Relationships were specified within the concept of havana, and these include two concentric circles: *havana lavidavitra,* who were distant but genealogically traceable by quite specific steps through familiar kin; and *havana akaiky,* who were close kin in two senses, (1) they were close genealogically and (2) they knew each other intimately irrespective of their genealogical relation. Havana lavidavitra was a category of kin who were always in the making, so to speak. When visiting abroad one might be interested in establishing a relationship with one's host, or one might come across people one had never met before. In both cases, after meeting people soon discussed their havana with each other, and if a relationship was discovered the parties recognized themselves as havana lavidavitra. It may also be that the genealogies stopped some distance from each other, but if two parties were mutually interested in establishing a connection, one might well be invented. Similar discussions took place when marriage negotiations had reached a serious stage, but here the purpose was to ascertain an absence or a distance of kinship connections, to ensure that if people were havana they were lavidavitra, not akaiky, since each foko (see later for discussion) had a rule of exogamy.

Havana was a general concept denoting a general status, and though it could be more tightly drawn as distant (lavidavitra) or close (akaiky), it did not, even in these specific forms, signify much of an instrumental function in the structuring of status or behavior. The sharper definition of the concept, and its activation, occurred when it was merged with spatial units. Thus there was havana akaiky plus *trano* (house), which defines a household (*ankohonana*), and havana akaiky plus *fizarana* (neighborhood), which defined the extended family circle (*fianakaviana*). This extended to people who had grown up together but who for reasons of emigration or marriage no longer lived intimately. The combination of several households that centered around a man, his brothers, and their sons, together with their wives and small children, functioned in the past as a solidary social unit known as *tokontrano*. Tokontrano was a commensal unit in which the wife of the senior male coordinated and supervised the work of her daughters-in-law and her own unmarried daughters in matters of food production, preparation, and consumption, thereby creating a sense of solidarity among the very people who were strangers to each other, namely fellow wives. This solidarity of tokontrano as expressed in the communal meal was known as *jao*. By 1963 the practice was in decline, though I visited several villages with tokontrano and jao. The sense of close bonding in the household and neighboring, kinship-related households was emphasized by the recognition of a unitary bond between certain pairs of relatives. *Mianaka* designated the close bond between parents and children; *mianadafy* the special bond between siblings and co-resident cousins; and *miafy* the bond of respect and familiarity between grandparents and grandchildren.

   Although ankohonana and fianakaviana were relatives whose closeness was reinforced by proximity, they were not "jural" groups with formal ritual or political status. The recognition of households as components of a neighborhood group depended on a specialized principle of havana, namely ascent (foko or karazana). Neither foko nor karazana meant ascent or descent but such a translation is implied, and I will return to the matter in a moment. The head of a household was usually the senior male, and his immediate neighbors in a section were usually his close male relatives (brothers, sons, father's brothers). These male relatives (havana akaiky) were recognized as a group with a common spiritual interest, unity in the same tomb, and the same ancestors, a status recognized by the designation *ambenilahy*. As males connected by their maleness laterally and lineally they were incorporated into a larger jural group concept that continued upward directly to the ancestors buried in the tomb. This was the fokondray, or karazana. Every section (fizarana) in a village (i.e., the spatial neighborhood, which formerly included tokontrano) was populated by ambenilahy and their wives. There were two capacities in which ambenilahy enjoyed a collective role: if they were of the foko whose tomb was in the nearby hills they were the guardians and trustees of that tomb on behalf of all the other members of the foko living abroad. In this role they became known as *mpiambinjana*. Their duties included hosting fellow foko members who had come to make special offerings to the ancestors in the tanindrazana, making offerings on behalf of fellow foko members who could not come themselves, making sure the ancestors were kept satisfied with regular offerings, and keeping the tomb dusted and tidy. The second role in which ambenilahy might be identified was as persons responsible for the village welfare, well-being, and order. In this capacity they were referred to as *tompontanana* (heads of the village). I have referred previously to the work groups (asareky), which were really groups whose full complement was based on the neighborhood because they included wives and children as well as resident and related males (i.e., ambenilahy). The equivalent status of the ambenilahy with respect to land when it was tompontanana and mpiambinjana was zafintany, i.e., those people of the foko who had the right to allocate the use of land among those who desired to cultivate it because they lived on the land of their ancestors (tanindrazana).

It is impossible to describe any further how I think Tsimihety organized themselves for action, and thought about themselves as being organized, without unpacking the idea of foko or karazana. Literally foko meant "of the same kind," and karazana meant something like common ancestry. Each of these synonyms catches a key aspect of the underlying concept. Foko was a term used to classify any sort of object into sets or categories, so foko when applied to people indicated a recognition of belonging to the same class or category and being distinct from other classes or categories. Karazana specified that the basis of such classification was common ancestry or, materially speaking, karazana-designated people who belonged to the same tomb. But this was more than just a classification. One's foko identity indicated a life trajectory that one shared with some and not with others. That community was a shared progress toward occupation of the same tomb, hence toward enjoying a shared community experience as ancestors together. At a more down-to-earth level sharing a foko identity was signalled by sharing various attributes and observances. People of the same foko observed the same taboos (*fady*); the same rule of exogamy; the same name and history; used the same earmark for cattle (*sofinomby*); the same customs, such as having, or not having, joking partners (*lohateny*) and having or not having the idea of a special rice field, the tanimbary omby; and in theory the same ancestors and the same tombs. People of the same foko also occupied the same status vis-à-vis the land on which they lived and which they grazed and cultivated. If the foko had its tomb in a faritany and was zafintany, then all the people who could identify themselves as being of that foko enjoyed zafintany status, whether or not they actually lived there.

Looked at from an individual's vantage point, each Tsimihety could identify himself either as *fokondray,* i.e., sharing the attributes of his father's foko, or *fokondreny,* sharing the attributes of his mother's foko. But the latter was in most instances a sort of shadow identity. Simply because everyone had a mother one was related, through her, to her fokondray. This was, though, a useful backup because in the event of a crisis or emergency or bad luck a man could be promised burial in the tomb of his mother's ancestors and hence consider himself as belonging to his fokondreny. When this happened his own children were as likely to consider their father's fokondreny as their own fokondray. So the natural priority was for an individual to be identified with his or her father's foko and with the line of ancestry that was housed in the tomb. I think this is the way Tsimihety looked at it, that is, as a line that they projected "upward" or "backward," a line of ascent rather than descent. People who shared the foko identity were people whose life careers were oriented in the same direction—ascending toward joining the same ancestors. It was this emphasis rather than an emphasis on viewing each other as descendants of the same ancestors that was stressed, even though people did recognize a common descent. Ascending into the tomb was the most important existential principle of the foko, and each individual, on the occasion of remembering or making offerings to the ancestors, cited a straight-line genealogy that reflected the shortest, most direct route back to the tomb. Even when meeting havana and trying to establish kinship links more precisely I got the impression (I cannot be certain) that every linking step was not traced out; it was enough to dart around citing most likely kinship links until a more or less direct route was established. Ascertaining kinship links during marriage negotiations was the only recurring occasion when precision was more or less at a premium.

During my travels I recorded 79 foko names, and during a session with a number of elders in Mandritsara 88 names were produced. The majority of these names shared the prefix *zafy,* grandchildren or descendants of, followed by a term that was not always a personal name but a term commemorating an event. For example: Zafindrarano, descendants of the water, commemorated a river crossing; Zafimita, descendants

of love charms. The other common prefix was *anti,* signifying a place
of origin, as in Antankavankina, Antailampy, and Antivohibe. Only in
very few instances was a foko name composed of the prefix followed by
a personal name, which suggests that foko name was probably not
intended to be even a symbolic designation for a group of descendants
of a common ancestor, let alone a literal designation. The term could
include those people whose ancestors shared a common experience, not
necessarily a common relationship. This supposition was in part suggested and in part confirmed when I entered a tomb and learned that
not all the occupants were related by kinship. There were the bones of
a man who had been rescued from Marofelana but who had died, a
woman who was described as *sakaiza* or lover, and the two "founders"
who I was told had become close friends when they had undertaken
several long and dangerous journeys together. The foko name was
zafizafotsy—the white descendants. On the other hand, the cave contained rows of coffins in varying states of decay, and each row, I was
told, comprised collateral relatives of succeeding generations. This was
a tomb in which both men and women were buried. Some tanindrazana
contain separate tombs for men and women. The tomb I visited had a
shadowy homogeneity, certainly not a rigorous or disciplined unity of
membership. I asked whether the ascending rows of coffins were "ambenilahy," that is, lineages. But I was told only that they were havana or
fokondray. At the time, and also when I sat down with elders in Mandritsara to talk about foko, I wanted to conceive of Tsimihety as being
lineage- and clan-based and to discover that foko were named groups
with some sort of corporate status. The hints enshrined in the notions
of foko and ambenilahy were tantalizing, and I was, at one time, tempted
to construct a model of "ideal types" and the approximation to them
represented "in reality." Such a model, apart from not reflecting what
Tsimihety said or did, would not work as a model when I tried to
formulate my idea of Tsimihety. Yet to abondon such pillars of ethnographic analysis was to leave me without the possibility of a positive,
structural analysis. I complained in print to people who did not have
structure (Wilson 1977). Foko were not structural groupings based on
descent that could be described by using a pyramidal model of nesting
boxes or branching lines. Foko was a term, identical to karazana, which
identified people with common attributes that included common kinship
through males (patrilineal ascent), but not only common ascent. These
attributes were prominent and important in establishing the priorities of

people to tombs, land, village, spouses, and, in special instances, friendship. People who were Zafimita, of the kind zafimita, were an association rather than a group. Other people were members of separate, but similar, associations, and everyone could have an honorary membership (through maternal kinship) in different associations. But a full membership was possible in the first instance in one's fokondray.

Foko were not exclusive or territorial and their members were scattered. But they did come together for reunions if they could, especially for funerals, famadihana, and weddings. But when they did, they did not assemble alone since members of other foko with ties of association also attended (lohateny, affines, friends, neighbors). When these reunions occurred a foko generally enjoyed the status of host, with all the obligations to provide hospitality and the right to be respected and to be shown gratitude. There was no hierarchy attached to a foko, no line of seniority or inherited position along which authority and responsibility were transmitted. Instead members of the association who gathered together were directed and managed in their ritual affairs by whoever among them was the senior member of the senior generation present. In a ritual capacity this was the mpijoro, and in a political capacity this was the soja. They were often the same person. The closer the affairs or the gathering got to the land of the tomb, the tanindrazana, the more fixed was the difference of status between those who habitually lived in the tanindrazana and maintained the tomb, mpiambinjana, and those whose residence was elsewhere. If the latter had no tomb of their own, they were ritually subordinate to the mpiambinjana. If they did have a tomb of their own they came to the land of their fellow foko as privileged guests, but would observe the ritual and political authority of the residents. No one was a member of a group that fitted together inside another one, or combined to create a larger one. And because individuals were members of the same association or foko they carried that identity with them. They were absorbed into the life of association members wherever they happened to be or meet up. No group, or its representatives, in other words, incorporated members into a larger whole in which their total social identities were interchangeable, or imposed upon individuals a transcendent collective authority. Tsimihety were not even a confederation of associations loosely joined under some fictive charter. Foko Tsimihety were simply associations that were based in Androna (and other regions), their bases being the tombs, and that shared the common attribute of "not cutting their hair," i.e., not recognizing hierarchical authority and organization. The associations were separate but equal, and their boundaries were not so much exclusive in intent as guidelines to provide existential direction in crucial matters relating to ancestorship, land allocation, and burial. Tsimihety in structural terms was an association of associations.

I am not alone in seeing a problem in understanding aspects of relating and classification in Madagascar or in trying to stretch and squeeze Malagasy fomba into African models. Aidan Southall has written of the debate about whether Malagasy kinship systems are agnatic or cognatic and has suggested that the debate is misconceived. He suggests that "it is not their qualities of cognation or agnation, but their emphasis on kinship and descent status as something achieved gradually and progressively throughout life, even after death, rather than ascribed and fixed at birth" (Southall 1986:417). He calls this "cumulative kinship." Providing the implications of something systematic and deliberate in this statement are not taken too literally, Southall's remark applies to the Tsimihety—in the sense that in a lifetime of moving around, people discovered kin, or redefined strangers as havana, or havana lavidavitra as havana akaiky. They aimed these journeys initially by means of kinship, which was always the platform on which an individual's life was based and from which it was launched.

It may not be proper to try to fit Tsimihety into a model applicable to the whole of Madagascar, because in 1963 the Tsimihety and their associational life may, in some ways, have been particular to them. As I have already suggested in the first chapter, there is evidence for a devolution of sociopolitical organization from one based at least on a weak political and ritual hierarchy to a life that was politically egalitarian. Second, there is some reason to think that the associational life, considered over time, represented a stratagem of political resistance to outsiders that has evolved more in blind fashion rather than as the result of political insight. Tsimihety were not the only people in Madagascar without chiefs or royalty. Bloch has described aspects of Zafimaniry egalitarianism. Zafimaniry, too, were threatened by conquest, but unlike Tsimihety were never in fact physically dominated because of the inaccessible terrain in which they lived (Bloch 1975:213). So their way of life was not determined in quite the same way by their relation to the outside. Tsimihety resisted an enemy who actually dwelt in their midst, and their resistance could not be based on total withdrawal and was not based on any threat of a resort to violence.

Returning to the applications of foko, some foko shared a relationship called *lohateny* or *tokondohateny,* which involved a form of joking. The origin of such a relationship between two foko usually was traced back to ancestors who rendered each other assistance at a vital time, such as rescue from enemies or disaster, or to ancestors helping each other out in times of crisis, such as providing cattle for preparing rice fields, or for an offering when the other was, for some reason, down on his luck and without his own cattle. Lohateny were pledged to mutual aid and assistance and to mutual hospitality; they considered it a good idea to exchange marriage partners, though there was no compulsion to do so. The most enjoyable feature of lohateny relationships was mutual cattle rustling. Lohateny might sneak up on their partners during the night, take some cattle, and then, before they departed, wake the village. Sleepy villagers rushed outside, made a lot of noise, and put up a lot of fake resistance as the raiders pretended to bloodthirsty attacks. Finally they retreated, taking cattle with them. Before long the attackers could expect to be the victims and the high jinks were repeated with the roles reversed. Any individual member(s) of a foko that was lohateny and who was receiving hospitality could expect to be the target of good-natured teasing and insults, but he or she could often return as "good as was got." Lohateny were, then, commemorative of personal histories that had grown to have social consequences, and the original events leading up to the agreement to establish lohateny were usually recalled during the course of a meeting. But to repeat, not all foko were lohateny, and the institution was not of universal political significance.

Foko identity was a background to marriage negotiations because every foko was distinguished by its exogamic specifications. Foko did not permit personnel to marry kin (havana) within various degrees of relationship, from three degrees to total prohibition. By degrees I mean reckoning a connection according to the number of generations upward one had to trace before being able to establish the collateral relationship. The prohibition did not define "descent/ascent" because it prohibited marriage with kin traced bilaterally, though matrilateral kin seemed to be less insistently prohibited. That was because matrilateral kin were likely to fade faster than patrilateral. Even when a prohibition extended to a total embargo it was not as imperative as it sounds, because if a relationship was discovered, even within reasonably close forbidden degrees, the disaster could be averted by offering an ox (*mandoza*) to remove the stigma and danger, i.e., to cancel out the kinship connection.

Tsimihety preferred to avoid endogamy because their political policy was to extend the reach and range of their connections, and marriage was a, if not the, most important way of doing this. But it was no great disaster if, occasionally, it turned out that people who married found out later they were already connected. Pressure was put on young people who knew they were connected and wanted to marry to find another spouse, but it was always possible for a couple to resist such pressure: if it came from the man's people the couple could live with the wife's people (a residence known as jaloko), or they could elope and live de facto (sakaiza) without going through a marriage ceremony. In both cases the man in particular was at a disadvantage. In the first instance, living with his wife's people, he had no authority over land or house. He was a vahiny. In the second instance both might have to live as strangers or try to make a go of it by homesteading. But these disadvantages were not insurmountable. I met a couple of men who lived jaloko and who enjoyed being "looked after." Their insecurity was not secular or economic but ritual in that the ancestors who ruled the land they lived on and who engaged in the day-to-day affairs of villagers were not *their* ancestors. If anything happened (illness, bad luck, bad dreams) jaloko were dependent on their male affines to intercede on their behalf with their, not the jaloko's, ancestors. In the allocation of land the jaloko did not have the priority and security of being zafintany, and while this may not have made too much difference economically it did make a difference psychologically. For when a man lived jaloko, he often lived beyond the cushioning company of familiar males with common interests in the important things in life, and, unlike fellow foko who may have emigrated, he had moved in a sort of defiance of his foko connections. Thus, the exception to the pattern of marriage residence revealed a prime sociological function of the foko: it provided an anchor and a lifeline, a sense of attachment and stability in an overall situation of constant movement and change. Thus "foko" was a stable reference point for the individual, especially for the male, wherever he moved, however far away he may have traveled from the tanindrazana. In the taboos (fadindrazana), the earmark (sofinomby), and the kinship encapsulated in the foko name, a Tsimihety person carried with him the credentials of a social and psychological identity that individualized and socialized inside the framework of being Tsmihety. The reality of this anchorage, identity and security were always there, objectified in the ancestral tomb. It is much like the assurance formerly provided by the promise on a bank note that it could be redeemed in gold if need be.

A foko included all those people who could trace their entry to the same tomb by links of patrilineal ascent. I find that very few of the genealogies I recorded contain the same names, which leads me to think that foko personnel were not bound by sharing the same ascent/descent links. These personal lines of ascent may well overlap and link up, but that was not a necessary feature. If they did, well and good. The thing that counted was that people traced their right of entry to the tomb so that their ancestors met there, so to speak. Because I find little or no evidence of connecting genealogies I cannot conclude that foko had a political significance as bounded and connected *groups*. Foko were not clans composed of lineages. In former times, this may have been the case if one accepts that some form of chieftainship existed (though lineage structure does not require that there be chiefs). Political groups with secular authority backed by ritual power do form an organization that could be seconded and utilized by conquerors seeking to administer their rule. The foko as it operated and functioned as I have described was a strictly private organization upon which no external government, be it French or other Malagasy, could get a grip.

Circumcision

Perhaps the best illustration of the secular, freewheeling attitude of Tsimihety was their approach to circumcision (*mamora zaza*). Elsewhere in Madagascar, circumcision is a central ritual, highly charged symbolically and of great political significance (particularly among the Merina as Bloch has brilliantly analyzed; Bloch 1986). Tsimihety circumcision was literally a "hit or miss" affair, and there were many Tsimihety men who were not circumcised at all.

The man who specialized in circumcising (known as *tsimijoro*) had no special qualifications other than the fact that he had learned the skill from another circumciser. As and when he felt like it in the dry season, the tsimijoro went off to a part of Androna and showed up in various villages. No one knew he was coming and when he arrived he was free to give notice that he would circumcise all the young boys he saw there who had not yet been circumcised. I was told by some men that he did not even have to tell the parents but would perform the operation on the spot. However, this is hard to accept since it often took two or more men to hold down a young boy about to be circumcised. This spontaneous circumcision was termed *kiso lehifitra*.

It was not accompanied by any ritual or any subsequent feasting or even celebration, though the boy was given good care. Tsimijoro did not have exclusive beats, but Tokonteny, the tsimijoro I knew best, said he usually confined his activities to villages around Marotandrano, to the south. He said he was paid about 100 francs and a chicken for each circumcision.

On some occasions the circumcision was more formalized. In the first place, the tsimijoro was invited by the father of the boy to come and perform the operation. At the same time the father invited his wife's brother, and each of them contributed a cow to the proceedings. The meat would form the basis of the feast given by the father to his havana akaiky and his wife's havana akaiky, i.e., his close affines. At night the women of both families sang for the happiness of the child; then, immediately before dawn, the operation was performed. The boy was brought out and held down by an older male (by the mother's brother on the occasion I watched). Special "powerful" water (*rano malaza*) was poured over the penis, after which the prepuce was marked with white earth; the foreskin was then drawn over till the ring passed the tip, and the tsimijoro severed the foreskin. He used an ordinary pocketknife specially sharpened, but with a wooden handle. Immediately after the foreskin had been cut off, it was handed to the mother's brother, who swallowed it in one gulp. (Alternatively he could throw it over roof of the house.) The tsimijoro spat salted water onto the wound, and bound it. After six days the boy was thrown into the river, or pond, where he bathed. After the circumcision the father and wife's brother symbolically grasped each other's beast by the hump before the animals were slaughtered and cooked for the meal, which was eaten the following day.

Compared with the elaborate and extended performance of Merina circumcision as described by Bloch, Tsimihety practice, while recognizably similar, was spare indeed. What is even more to the point was that most of the circumcisions performed did not follow this ritual procedure at all, and, secondly, many men were *never* circumcised. If a boy passed his fourth year without having been spotted by a tsimijoro, or if his father was not interested or generous enough to call in the tsimijoro, it was certain that he would grow up uncircumcised.

It might be argued that all this testified to the changing nature of

Tsimihety culture; rituals that were prominent and imperative in the past were fading in 1963. Circumcision in 1963 was better described as optional, as illustrating the degrees of freedom people gave themselves to conform to the past, or to obey contingency, or to announce adherence to change. The optional nature of circumcision certainly removed from it any universally accepted and authenticated symbolic relevance it might have had for power relations. The lack of organization of circumcision exemplified in the almost random forays of the tsimijoro, and in the fact that Tsimihety admitted many men were uncircumcized, reflected, if it reflected anything at all, the rejection by Tsimihety of symbols and rituals of power inherent in Malagasy culture as a whole. In this sense, the parallel between the purported refusal of Tsimihety in the past to observe rituals of royal mourning and their informal attitude to circumcision was consistent with their emphasis on equality and liberty.

Marriage (*Fanambadiana*)

Politically, marriage could be expansive (exogamy) or exclusive (endogamy), and, in both cases, marriage ensured the continuity of kinship. I have already indicated the expansive nature of Tsimihety marriage. People tended to expand their network of connections by marrying people who previously were unrelated and/or marrying people living some distance away. I had thought, when I was in the field and when I tried to write up, that the majority of couples living together were formally married and that young people wanted to get married. Now I am not so sure that this was the case. There is evidence in my notes that pressure was sometimes brought to bear on young people to marry someone suggested, or preferred, by an older kinsperson. Several people, men and women, told me that they did not know each other very well before they were married. Their parents, or in some cases an older sibling, wanted the marriage. In one case a man said to me he had needed a woman to cook his meals, and his older brother had contacted a family in a distant village. The girl was only thirteen, and although she came to live with my informant, they had not been happy and she had gone back to her parents. But the strongest query about the necessity of marriage was the fact that the universal form was *fanambady miletry* or moletry, which involved payment of a bride-price and which everyone said was recent; it was also undergoing extensive modification during my stay, because trial marriages (*jofa*) were becoming more and more frequent. Though I would have needed to check directly, I suspect now that many couples, who often lived together for years, were not in fact married in any ceremonial or ritual sense. Some admitted they were sakaiza (friends) but I suspect there were many more. This leads me to think that the conjugal relationship was much more open and less binding than we are accustomed to think of it, especially when rituals binding "groups" together are involved and when great expense is involved in putting on ceremonials. The stability of a marital relationship depends on emotional compatibility rather than formal structural ties. Children convert the weaker ties of affinal relationship into the stronger ties of cognatic kinship, and that is what is important.

Having expressed these reservations about my own understanding of marriage among Tsimihety as reflected in the inadequacies of my notes I can go on to discuss what I took to be the paradigm of marriage.

Sexual relations between young unmarried people were quite free, there being only a relatively informal restriction on sexual contact between male and female belonging to the same village. Adolescents were left quite free to have sexual relations with visitors, and were provided with an empty house. Sometimes sexual hospitality was provided for visitors. In theory young people eventually found someone they would like to marry. Parents were informed, and parents informed senior kin. This set in motion a process of discrete inquiry by relatives on both sides who tried to find out, first, whether there already existed a kinship relation between the two individuals, then whether the households and extended family (fianakaviana) were diligent or slovenly and whether the prospective spouse was likely to have been brought up well to perform his or her role. The usual method of making such inquiries was to contact a kinperson who was likely to know the prospective spouses and their families. But dissembling visits would also be made—a father might go to ostensibly look for cattle for his collection, or pretend to be on his way to another village, and then find an excuse to stop off at the prospect's village. Otherwise, these same contacts and inquiries might be used to come up with a suggested match that they think will be advantageous. Then the problem was to convince the young prospects. They were encouraged to spend time together and, depending on how strong the respective fianakaviana thought such a match would be, they tried to persuade the young couple. If the couple was not agreeable, they could not be forced, and if the couple wanted to live together they could elope. Usually it was the girl who did not want to marry, in which case she might bow to pressure by living with the man for a short while, then leave him.

Assuming all had gone well and both sides received good reports from their spies, formal approaches were made by the boy's immediate kin, and each stage of negotiation was marked by an exchange of small gifts. The negotiations centered around the amount of the miletry, which consisted of cattle and money. I have no record of any miletry exceeding five head of cattle with two thousand francs. Not only the number of cattle was negotiated but also their type (age, coat color and pattern, horns, etc.). Then agreement had to be reached on the number of people who would make up the *mpaka,* the group that escorted the groom to the bride's village (and who had to be ostentatiously fed), and the *mpanatitra,* the cortege that escorted the bride to her husband's village (and which also had to be properly entertained). At one wedding, which I attended, the bride's people were thrown into a complete tizzy because the mpaka numbered 43 when they were expecting only 25. There was no time to kill another ox, which they were unwilling to do, so the women frantically chased down chickens and geese. Although there was much groaning and threats of cancelling the wedding among the bride's people, when the mpaka arrived they were all smiles and put on a show as if they had not been in the least fazed. During the speeches, though, I caught several remarks about how good it was to stick to promises. On another occasion, at the handing over of the miletry, two animals did not pass inspection. The formality of the proceedings broke down as the arguments heated up. But in the end the animals were substituted. On both sides in a wedding, there seemed to be a degree of gamesmanship, each side seeing what it could get away with. This was true of other times when Tsimihety dealt in cattle.

A woman's close kin, havana akaiky, were informed of her marriage and were expected to send presents. Each donation was announced during the feast at the bride's village before she left for her husband's village, and it formed part of her dowry (meomeo). The young men and girls who took her to her husband's village also helped to carry the meomeo, which consisted of goods and chattels to set up a home. One meomeo I was able to inventory consisted of 40 baskets, 21 mats, an enamel coffeepot, 6 enamel plates, 6 cups and 6 saucers, 10 glasses, 10 pillows, 1 bolster, a castiron cooking pot, a kettle, 4 measures (*sobiki*) of rice, spoons and forks, a ladle, a box of matches, a bar of soap, a pail, a suitcase, a trunk, 2 umbrellas, 12 dresses, an oil lamp, and 715 francs.

Besides the young people who escorted the bride and groom, the fianakaviana of each spouse attended the celebrations in each village. The elders of the host village were involved in the entertainment and especially in the *kabary,* or speech making. These speeches included proverbs and sayings, but were usually quite short and unelaborate, tending to emphasize the advantages to both sets of kin of the new union, and how pleased everyone must be. When a bride entered her husband's village she was led to the tompontrano, the house of the senior male of the village, and he together with the rayamandreny or elders asked her why she had come, and then instructed her in the fady of the village and its foko.

Most people with whom I discussed the subject seemed to think that such formal miletry marriages were risky and expensive because people were exploiting the fact that (1) the woman always retained ownership of the meomeo, and (2) once the miletry had been paid, the bride, with the encouragement of her family, increasingly tended to walk out of the marriage after a year. So, to counter this, trial marriages (dia jofa) were preferred. A couple set up house together, and if, after one or two years, children had been born and the union seemed stable, then the ceremonies were held and the miletry handed over. The advantage of miletry over other, less formal unions, was that it brought together two unrelated groups of kin in an explicitly political sense. The trial marriage, or the de facto marriage, relied on the individual partners, and the alliance of kin networks was never established. It might happen slowly and irregularly, as visiting took place.

This generalized description of marriage and conjugal partnership shows that on balance the individual retained a freedom of choice, he or she being always free to go his or her own way. But this was modified to accommodate the desires of other people to whom one was close to extend kinship networks and hence lines of possible migration and mobility. This was not the "function" of marriage, nor can marriage be said to have been the means of an alliance between two political and territorial groups. Rather marriage was in part a service that individuals could perform for others under varying degrees of pressure, as well as for themselves. Groups did not view marriage as the means to recruit new members, because there were no political groups involved, but individuals did consider formal marriage, with bride-price, the means to guarantee the achievement of their own ancestry. When men spoke of their sons belonging to them, they always spoke of the assurance they had that there would be someone to bury them, to exhume them, to install them in the tomb, and to continue to make offerings to them. They never spoke, as far as I am aware, of ensuring the continuance of the group (the ambenilahy or the fokondray). A woman was always assured of a proper burial either by her paternal relatives, or, in some cases, by her husband in his family tomb. A man was never secure in the knowledge that he would be buried with his paternal ancestors unless he had sons. Yet, even if he had not married with miletry and assured himself of sons to bury him, to carry the line forward, he could hand over to the mother of his child and her immediate kin a small payment (*valy tarina*) of about 300 Malagasy francs or a cow when the child was between three and seven years old, and this child enjoyed all the rights and assumed all the obligations of fokondray. This could happen with children born of casual unions among young people (*zazatany*), of de facto (sakaiza) relationships, and of couples where the man was living in his wife's village (jaloko). In the latter case a miletry could also be negotiated. If the valy tarina was not paid, the children accompanied their mother, and if she married they were distinguished from her other children as *zaza manandreny*. They could expect to cultivate land and be buried in their mother's tanindrazana, and for ritual identification were identified as fokondreny.

Individuals, even though married, were relatively free to engage in extramarital unions and to have lovers (sakaiza). A number of instances of polygamous households came to my notice. In one case the man had three wives, each living in separate villages, and mistresses living in their own homes. Only one of these wives lived in her husband's village. In another instance a man lived with four wives, each with her separate hut but sharing a kitchen in a homestead situation. As well, individuals were free to engage in sororate (*soatrano*) or levirate (*vono afo*), and as far as I could make out such arrangements were entered into for purely individual motives of compassion and sympathy. The distinction between children born as successors to their father and children, especially sons, whose place remained with the mother was shown in the practice of *teknonymy*. A man assumed the title "father" plus his name, for the son who would bury him, but not if this was not to be the case. A father's father marked his elevation toward ancestorship by incorporating into his title the name of a grandson. Teknonymy underlined the ascent of males and females rather than the descent of their offspring.

Though the miletry marriage was, at the time of my fieldwork, undergoing change, it was regarded by all as being the orthodox form of marriage. Miletry marriage involved the handing over by the husband (and his close kin) of up to five head of cattle and up to 2,000 Malagasy francs. Everybody told me that in the event of a divorce, a woman would give back all, or part, of the miletry depending on how many children had been born to the union, i.e., cattle were regarded as being exchanged for the fertility of the woman, a capacity that was unavailable to the men from among his own kin, by virtue of the rules of exogamy and against incest.

This would suggest that, formally speaking at least, males depended on females as wives for ensuring their social perpetuation, i.e., that women were more important to men as wives than as sisters.

Conclusion

Anyone traversing Androna would see a few villages by the roadside, but would miss the majority of villages set well off any identifiable road. The villages one could see appeared well-established, and the houses of mud, dung, and thatch looked sound and solid—not like the flimsy reed and raphia huts that people say they used to live in, and of which there were still a few in some villages. All the villages had essentially identical plans. One or two "streets" at an angle northeast/southwest, on both sides of which stood larger rows of huts. From some smoke curled up out of the thatch or the doorway. A few had small lean-tos at the side, or even separate thatch huts that were the kitchens. Then, there were outer rows of granaries, some on stilts, others on the ground but with entry from on top. Some villages looked in better shape than others, and it was not unusual to come across abandoned, near derelict houses or even crumbling villages. Villages were rarely very big, usually less than a dozen houses. But there were a few with around a hundred houses still set out in parallel rows. On the whole, expecially when set amidst the bright green of ripening rice, a stranger got the impression of comfortable and well-settled people—good peasant stock.

If, however, you tried to find your way according to the map issued by the Service Geographique in 1958 (scale 1:100,000) you constantly came across villages not marked on the map; vice versa, many villages named on the map seemed not to exist, and to never have existed, for there was no trace of them. It was simply the case that, though the houses were solid and the villages seemed permanent, Tsimihety never felt committed to stay in one place and did not identify themselves with a place of birth or residence. Houses and villages would be abandoned at the slightest pretext (though usually on the advice of the ombiasa). Formerly they were always abandoned after a death had occurred, and often after a severe illness. In 1963, people were as likely to move for these reasons, though they did not always feel they had to. My point is that considered geographically, demographically, or economically, or in any materialistic way, Tsimihety were mobile seminomadic people. Through this mobility they could express their sense of freedom and defiance of outside authority because they could always exercise what Albert O. Hirschman has called the "exit option."

But in a spiritual, nonphysical, social sense Tsimihety were stable, cohesive, and firmly founded. The mechanism of this foundation of stability was the entire complex of kinship and the forms in which it was expressed. Basically, kinship ties could always be invoked to keep up connections independently of residence or geographical proximity—independently because ownership of property was not so much a legal consideration as it was a spiritual or ancestral one. When people left a house, village, or land they abandoned the material form but retained the intangible right to house, village, or land. Rather than the village or house, the anchor for any Tsimihety individual was the tomb and its inhabitants. The tomb was hidden and the ancestors invisible—only their bony remains being evident. Nothing then, least of all outsiders, could upset this foundation of individual and social identity and cohesiveness. The constant visiting as well as the more periodic exchanges and visiting were significant not only for sustaining physical contact but also for perpetuating and activating the spiritual or metaphysical aspects of kinship that centered around the dead and the ancestors. Again, the independence of kinship from residence was important because it was a tie that could not be interfered with by outside forces. One could, for example, tax or recruit households or villages, but not people who were bound by kinship. So, if the taxman came it was no hardship to abandon house and village because the "community" to which one belonged was the open network of kin. This was not a corporate or shaped community so much as it was a continually changing set of options from which to choose where to go, who to live with, who to marry, what lands to cultivate, or which pastures to graze. One did not, of course, choose one's kin, but through marriage it was often the case that one chose who should become kin and affines (the same term, havana, was used for cognates and affines). Individuals could choose their own particular quasi kin; their blood brothers (fati-dra) and another form of quasi kin, lohateny, was the outcome of voluntary and mutual choice. Friendship, too, was prominent among Tsimihety, and this was often treated as, or converted to, kinship. So kinship, in its numerous forms, was the axis around which both the social and political sympathies of Tsimihety revolved—but precisely for reasons of its invisibility rather than for the usually cited reasons that it provided the criteria for establishing the exclusive boundaries of political and territorial groups. No conqueror, administrator, or functionary could see, or know, a kinship tie and so could not easily find people or pin them down. But Tsimihety knew very well who were their kin and where they could go if need be to avoid outside oppression. Or, if oppression was not the issue, each individual had his or her own web of kin and could select which strand to follow as needs suggested.

Kinship provided the network of relationships within which the individual received the stimulus for and confirmation of the performance of actions that were personally fulfilling; at the same time, however, it provided the individual with a sense of belonging. This is in contrast to capitalist freedom, for example, where confirmation and recognition of fulfillment was usually in market or monetary terms. In terms of liberal philosophy the context of kinship was the context that marshalled people into positions from which they could contribute to each others' well-being. There were obligations associated with kinship and ascent, but here one might argue that the presence of such duties only helped to clarify the existence of personal freedom: their performance was the substance of that freedom. Kinship was a set of options that could be taken up, or rejected, by individual Tsimihety. People could choose to live with some kin and leave other kin; kin were the guidelines along which individuals exercised their even more basic freedom to move. This freedom to move in turn was made meaningful, rendered purposeful and self-conscious, by virtue of the basic defining dichotomy—Tsimihety versus outsiders. By consciously defining their goals in terms of a resistance to the outside, Tsimihety asserted or made themselves aware of their moral autonomy. What they did, who they chose to relate to, or live with, was their *own* choice and hence they were free.

Kinship, which is so often seen by ethnographers and theorists drawing from ethnography as a symptom of constraint and restriction, can in fact be the source of liberation. In the most general sense, the

distinction of kin establishes the grounds for a basic choice between kin
or nonkin (family or occupational role). And then, in the Tsimihety
case, kinship established the grounds for choice between some kin and
other kin.

CHAPTER 5

Power

When I carried out fieldwork on the Caribbean island of Providencia I was always impressed by the trouble people took to dress immaculately on Sunday when they attended church. I was awed somewhat by the seriousness and commitment preacher, priest, and congregation showed in church. The elaborate and expensive preparations of food for display and consumption at weddings and the abandonment of people to the joy of the moment, or the sadness, seemed to me appropriate to the separateness of ritual from everyday life. It was the same in the Malay village in which I also lived and worked. The echoes of this awe continued to sound in the respect ordinary people had for the officiants outside of the ritual occasion, and I, too, approached them with a degree of respectful hesitancy. And for that matter I recall being overawed almost to the point of fear by the precision, solemnity, discipline, and otherworldliness of religious services I attended. My own wedding was designed differently, yet it was meticulously planned and executed; no one, least of all the groom, was left in any doubt as to the sheer naked "reality" of the occasion as something forever and as something out of the ordinary. However, ritual and its attendant ceremonials may be analyzed and classified, and whatever they may be interpreted as saying and doing, it seems as if they always try to reveal or lead back to the powers that awe and cower people, at least for the moment. This affect of ritual is what is meant, I think, by referring to its connection with the sacred and the sublime.

I am not attempting here to insist on any general principles of explanation. I am simply trying to provide a background for my expectations of, and reactions to, Tsimihety ritual. To put it bluntly, what I thought was ritual and ceremonial among Tsimihety left me quite unimpressed. I had no feeling of being present among people who were touched by the sacred and the sublime. The offerings of cattle, the invocations, the speeches, promises, and requests made to spirits and ancestors were barely set apart from normal everyday life. No one dressed up, no one seemed awed, even the officiants said and acted quite matter of factly, as they might have been commenting on the weather at breakfast. Even in the tomb, there in the presence of the ancestors who were always spoken of as the fountainhead, no one behaved as if they were present in a sacred and powerful place. Cleaning and tidying, rearranging and general inspection were carried out much as if one was tidying up the hut. When animals were sacrificed young men wrestled with them beforehand, laughing, joking, and cursing. Then, when the animal slumped to the ground with tiredness, the mpijoro said a few words and one of the men slit its throat with a machete that had been specially sharpened beforehand. The blood was caught, but in an ordinary bucket and with no sense of urgency or a felt need to do it properly. The only occasions in which a separate reality was intimated was when tromba went into trance. But even then many people in the audience seemed to treat it more as entertainment than as a communication with the supernatural.

Both my own personal and fieldwork experiences, as well as theoretical discussions of "ritual" in anthropological literature, conditioned me to think of it as having to be separate, formal, awesome, fraught with layers of meaning, and above all to be that form of human behavior preeminently concerned with the unfathomable depths of power. Such conditioning, which asserted in essence that the form was function, has been quite thrown into confusion by Tsimihety and by my recordings of them. By freeing myself from this conditioning, not by any intellectual or emotional effort on my part, but simply thanks to the passage of time, I can see how I might be able to describe, and perhaps explain, how Tsimihety ritual was incorporated into Tsimihety life, and particularly into their total contextual situation.

Ritual, of course, is so exotic and hence so appealing and challenging to anthropologists that it often forms the centerpiece of an ethnographic study as well as being the subject of ingenious and sophisticated theorizing. It is difficult, then, to appreciate the possibility that for some people, for whatever reason, ritual is a devalued or undervalued form of activity. But this is the case and at least one ethnographer, Fredrik Barth, has confronted such a situation among the Basseri, a nomadic tribe in southern Persia. He writes:

The Basseri show a poverty of ritual activities which is quite striking in the field situation; what they have of ceremonies, avoidance customs, and beliefs seem to influence, or be expressed in, very few of their actions. What is more, the different elements of ritual do not seem closely connected or interrelated in a wider system of meanings; they give the impression of occurring without reference to each other, or to important features of the social structure. (Barth 1961:135)

Tsimihety certainly performed ritual activities—largely forms of offerings to ancestors and spirits, observance of taboos (fady), and programmatical ways of marking life-cycle events. But they did not seem to have either a ritual "mind" or a ritual "attitude." Procedures were not consistent, were often optional, largely depending on individuals. There was no uniform social pressure to perform ritually, and when acts were performed ritually it was without fuss, without being set apart, without special preparation. The only officiant was the mpijoro, but other than doing most of the speaking, he was indistinguishable from the rest. He was not a specialist and knew no more, often less, than the others. There is another similarity between Basseri and Tsimihety. The Basseri are fully nomadic pastoralists and, according to Barth, the supreme value for them is not so much owning lots of cattle but having the freedom to migrate (Ibid.:149). Freedom as autonomy and independence, in which migration plays a significant part, was possibly the supreme value for Tsimihety as well. In saying this we have to be clear that what I think this means is not simply a collective freedom, i.e., Tsimihety as a polity free to manage its own affairs, because there was no Tsimihety polity. Tsimihety freedom was freedom from the institutional instruments of constraint, and power. This meant, in particular, freedom from any semblance of an all-inclusive hierarchy, be this externally imposed or internally generated, and from ritual, political, and jural hierarchies in which may be vested the power to determine or interfere with any and all aspects of life. This did not exclude the possibility of "private" or "personal" hierarchies that could assume specific responsibilities, and hence powers, useful at different times to the individual in guiding and assisting him or her along a smooth "life course." Tsimihety did not seem to regard this life course as inevitable and out of their hands. No supreme deity assured its fulfillment by taking a special interest in each individual. Rather, life was constantly threatened by problematic influences like illness, and uncertainties, to which one had to react or manage.

Life began in uncertainty, and the first few months were very risky. So much so that, in order to deter spirits and illness, a child was given an unflattering name (such as *diky,* shit, or *sofinmena,* red ears or European), to deceive malicious spirits. Once survival seemed likely, after the cutting of the first tooth, the hair was shaved and a new name was conferred. Illness was a constant threat to survival, and all undertakings were subject to risk and failure; every ambition and intention of the living was a reaching out into the unknown that had to be both guarded against and assured as best as one could. But there were means of management at one's disposal. Death, of course, was certain, but incomplete. Complete death ensconced an insecure, wandering ancestor in the tomb, ensuring the fulfillment of a life in ancestorship. A person must have children, especially sons, to ensure burial, but only the birth of grandchildren put the achievement of ancestry beyond doubt. Even then there was the worry (and it was very real) that one's descendants would not live up to their duty of ensuring a restful sojourn in the tomb. Many illnesses and much bad luck was attributed to the dissatisfaction of the recently dead with the performance (or lack) of propitiatory duties. There was something that could be done, and other things that had to be done, to help an individual across and through the "life course." Most of these things required other people, often people with special skills and talents, special powers even. But those skills, talents, and powers were activated only when needed and on behalf of clients. They were not regarded or treated as elevating their possessors to permanent power, so they could never become powerful and hence achieve positions of rank. The irrelevance of rank (or the danger of it) to Tsimihety may perhaps explain why rituals were undemonstrative, uncostumed, unelaborate, and without paraphernalia. They were not allowed to denote any power beyond that for which they had been convened.

So much, then, by way of general introduction to that part of my account that has to reconcile Tsimihety liberty, equality, and fraternity with the presence of power in their lives.

Burial

It is fair to say, I think, that Tsimihety regarded a proper burial as the most unqualifiedly imperative requirement in a person's life cycle: birth and early maturation were noted with care and private precautions were made to ensure survival; circumcision was optional; marriage was both optional and variable; illness, as I shall discuss, was a central consideration for all Tsimihety; and the secondary burial of an exhumed body, while desirable, was optional and often informal. Only the funeral and burial of a person was an event that had to be performed in a properly prescribed manner, i.e., as a ritual.

Velo died, quite unexpectedly, at 7:30 A.M. Within fifteen minutes of his expiry two of his sons, and his younger brother, carried him outside. All the men in the village, having been notified, were building a raphia shelter between Velo's granaries. Three young men made a bier out of raphia branches. Still in the open, the sons and brother washed the body and wrapped it in a white shroud or lamba and then laid it on the bier (*kobanafaty*) in the mourning house (*tranovorana*), where it was hidden from view by curtains. The builders erected a thatch roof over an area covered by mats on which mourners would sit. When this had been completed, the older women, who had been secluded in the house, took their place around the tranovorana, and the men gave way (women with young children and menstruating women had to remain in the house).

While all this was going on young children had been sent out to neighboring villages to report on Velo's death. Velo's eldest son had selected two beasts from his father's herd, which had been led away and killed. Within three hours of Velo's death the first visitors began arriving, mostly young men. They joined the local young men in butchering the animals and cooking the meat. The young women and girls had been pounding rice and were helped by young men (every village household donated at least one bidon (an eight-liter can) of rice as a gift (*fitia tsimbahetry*). The same name was given to the small money gift given by visitors as they arrived. Their names were entered into a book, if there was someone present who could write.

New arrivals kept coming through the night. As they neared the village women began wailing and were then greeted by the widow, who emerged from the hut wearing her white lamba. The men were greeted by Lehova, who had succeeded Velo. Older men and women sat apart but around the corpse while younger adults assisted with cooking. In this case nine large pots were used for the rice. When one pot was cooked, the rice was stuffed into a raphia sack to keep hot until it was time to eat. The meat was cut up small; the old men ate a small piece of liver first and the heads of the animals were then put on posts at the east end of the head of the corpse.

At about 12:30 P.M. the following day all the men sat down to eat. They sat in two rows facing each other with bowls of rice and meat placed alternately between them. The women ate separately and the older women ate in the tranovorana. The younger men and women were free to eat at any and all times they were engaged in cooking. The men were allowed to spear meat and roast, a practice not allowed at any other time because it was associated with death. Alcohol (wine and fermented rum or betsabetsa) was available all the time.

It so happened that on this, the second day, another death occurred in a neighboring village of one of Velo's kinsmen. It was agreed that both men would be buried at the same time, though in different places. Thus, the actual interment was postponed until the third day. At about 10:30 A.M. on the third day the women moved out of the tranovorana and the men moved in. They removed the curtains and wrapped the body in a green cloth tied with seven cords. The tying was done by young men under the close and concerned direction of the old men, all of whom were issuing orders about the tying at the same time. The body was then placed on a mat, which was tied with four cords, and, again, there was much shouting and concern for the tying. The body was then replaced on the bier and covered with a white shroud, which was not tied.

The funeral procession then began. The four pallbearers were younger men, but new bearers took over every few minutes or so. As soon as the bier was lifted, the women wailed for the last time. The bier was preceded by young boys carrying the impaled ox heads and an ox heart, which was thrown away when the corpse had been buried. Men and women marched separately, but took turns to march in the front or the rear of the procession. The elders tended to be silent, but the young men especially were often quite rowdy.

The grave itself was a hollowed out space beneath a huge rock halfway up a hillside, about six kilometers from the village. Several young men, now getting drunk, swept out the grave and were given more rum. The bier was lowered, the cords were cut, and the green cloth and the bier were thrown down the hill. The corpse was then wrapped in a white shroud (*lamba mena*), left untied, and then other young men placed the body in the hole with the head to the east. Alongside were placed: Velo's two jackets, his hat, two plates (one china, one enamel), one enamel mug, a spoon, a glass, his pocketknife, his cane (*koboay*), and about thirty-five francs.

Under the direction of Velo's eldest son the grave was sealed up with stones very carefully. Lehova, now mpijoro, poured a cup of bet-sabetsa over the stones and told the ancestors (*razana*) that Velo had come to join them. While he was doing this, the eldest son read out the statistics of the burial: number of cows eaten (3), number of liters of alcohol consumed (46), number of bidons of rice consumed (11), total amount of money contributed (1383 ariary, or 6,195 francs), and, finally, number of people present (167).

After the burial everyone returned to their respective villages. The only subsequent happening was that eight days later, Lehova announced to the women of Andilamena that they could now tress their hair again, having let it down from the time mourning began.

This was a ritual procedure in which everyone knew their parts so that there was minimal organization required. People slipped into their roles as mourners as a matter of course. No individual assumed either ritual or organizational preeminence, and the only notable distinctions were those that were evident in ordinary Tsimihety activity: distinctions between senior and junior, and between male and female. Such symbolism as was evident was inherent in Malagasy culture as a whole, for example, white as the color of mourning, though in the Tsimihety case the dead were wrapped in a white shroud and the wearing of white by mourners was optional. The positioning of the body (head to the east) and the loosening of tresses by females were typical of Malagasy burial in general.

Even in burial, which was the most ritualized of Tsimihety proce-dures, there was no evidence of a differentiation of political powers and of their buttressing in symbolic expression. Knowledge was not spe-cialized, and authority was diffused. Any individual role was essentially managerial but was not the province of a specialist. It was rather the responsibility of kin.

Though not disruptive of personal relations (there were no inquests, no accusations of witchcraft) death could disrupt the flow of life. The house in which a death had occurred was left vacant for at least some time. In earlier times it was burned down, and it was still likely that people might decide to move out of a village in which a death had occurred, particularly the death of a younger person.

It was unfortunate that I was never present at a "legal" *famadihana*.

The only one that I witnessed was an illegal one, one which took place during the rainy season and involved the exhumation of an infant who had died only 18 months earlier. By government order famadihana should take place only in the dry season and corpses must have been buried at least three years. It is more than likely that such a famadihana was shorn of many of its public aspects.

The main purpose of famadihana was to transfer the remains of the dead from a grave to the ancestral tomb and to place the bones that had become disconnected into a coffin where they could remain integrated. Once in the tomb the coffins were not usually removed again (as, for example, is the case with the Merina famadihana), though they might be subject to some tidying up. The coffins were made of hardwood and shaped like a house.

The famadihana at which I was present was initiated because Vonda and his family had been suffering from unexplained and as yet uncured illnesses for the past six months. The ombiasa had diagnosed that his infant son, who had died some 18 months earlier, was irritable and restless because he had not yet joined the ancestral tomb. This diagnosis was confirmed by a second ombiasa. A small offering of rum was made at the ancestral altar in the village, and the ancestors were assured by Vonda that he would immediately attend to the installation of his son. The exhumation was planned for Saturday (a favorable day) until it was discovered that this would be in the phase of the new moon (unfavorable). The exhumation was postponed until Monday.

With no ceremony, Vonda, his two younger brothers, and myself left the village in mid-afternoon, climbed halfway up a hill about five kilometers away, and Vonda dug up the remains from beneath a rock. These he wrapped in a raphia cloth, which he tied loosely. We then proceeded to the summit, walking across the ridge to the next hill where the tomb was situated. Vonda sprinkled a little rum in front of the cave entrance and perfunctorily announced: "We have come with the remains of Rakoto." We all moved brush and rocks aside and entered the tomb. Vonda looked around and walked to a coffin, which he opened; adjudging there was room inside, he placed the wrapped remains of his infant son inside, replaced the lid, poured a little rum, and said, simply, "Thank you." After this we all drank a little rum. In the fast-fading light (famadihana must take place when the sun is going down), the men wandered around the cave, tidying up. Not all bones were in coffins and where bones had scattered when the shrouds had finally given way, they were regrouped. The occupants of some of the coffins were remembered and became the subject of remarks and stories. But with darkness quickly approaching the entrance to the cave was resealed, and we began our return to the village. Other than this there was no celebration, no special meal, and no further ritual.

During the dry months Tsimihety transferred the dead from graves to the tombs. This transfer was done very matter of factly, and whether kin were gathered to partake of a ceremonial meal seemed to be optional. Unfortunately I did not observe such an event, and my discussions with Tsimihety about famadihana were not as detailed as perhaps they should have been.

Health and Illness: Diagnosis and Advice

The most worrying and constant threat to individual freedom and well-being was illness. I did not investigate Tsimihety ideas about illness to any depth and can make no pretense to offer either a detailed examination or satisfactory account of their theories of health and illness. There seemed to be a division between symptoms, which were physical and were treated physically through the prescription of medicines made from plants with known healing properties, and causes, which were supernatural. Medicines were often prescribed during the course of the examination to ascertain the supernatural causes of the illness. There was also a preventive medicine, manifested chiefly in the wearing of amulets of beads and string, these having been purchased from the ombiasa. Most women and children, and some men, wore such amulets, which among other things testified to the frequency with which ombiasa were consulted. Prevention, or at least preemption, was also sought by the continual making of small offerings to spirits and ancestors during the course of the daily routine. Such measures did not require the services of a special officiant. Most Tsimihety houses had a small device of two or three wooden tubes hanging in the rafters and known as *talatala*. These were filled with honey and were kept topped up as a permanent offering to spirits to divert their attention from the occupants, upon whom they might bring some ailment. The senior male of the household was usually responsible for this. Whenever Tsimihety journeyed forth, which was frequently, they would perhaps build a roadside altar or place a small offering on an existing altar (*tsangambato*) of flowers, rice, or cloth so as to ensure a safe journey and to prevent illness and mishap.

A large number of symptoms, such as runny nose, sore throat, constipation, earache, toothache, headaches, and, for women, menstrual pains and cramps, could be treated initially by the sufferer or, if a child, by the adults of the household. Most Tsimihety, as far as I could gather, knew a number of standard treatments, *odindrazana* (ancestral medicines), for such ailments. Most of these were herbal (Tsomangamena was a good purge; hazomboay was also good; green tobacoo leaf soaked in water was good for sore eyes; pounded spinach leaves (*anamalao*) were good for earache; boiled raphia bark was good for toothache; colds were treated by inhaling the fumes from an infusion of the *romba* herb, and so on).

In the first instance, then, most people treated themselves or were treated by close kin and no "professionals" were involved. The patient, the illness/injury, the medicine, and the administrator were all conjoined as a cognitive unity. It was when symptoms did not respond to these personal treatments that people had to go outside the circle of immediate kin and think beyond the original unity; it was then that they entered into a client/authority relationship with a specialist, the ombiasa or the *mpisikidy,* the diviner (the two were often the same person). Engagement in such a relationship occurred regularly when enterprises failed, and there was a need to know why. This was especially so when the client had taken all precautions to ensure success, particularly by promising to offer an ox to the ancestors and the spirits in return for success (a promise known as *manalatsikafara*). This was when the outside authority, the ombiasa, was called in and the range of ritual reference was shifted beyond the individual and "public" knowledge to the expert (ombiasa) and proprietary knowledge (*sikidy*). The treatment became a public event at which not just members of the household were involved but all members of the segment, who had to be fed. These public offerings (joro) were politically structured rather than domestically structured because they mustered together a congregation recruited by shared descent and/or residence under the particular ritual authority of the mpijoro, the senior male of the senior generation of the sector involved (*ankohonana, ambenilahy*).

There was an alternative to consulting the ombiasa when illness prevailed, or when failure predominated. This alternative was to consult the tromba. Whereas consultations with the ombiasa are always private, between patient and doctor, consultation with the shaman is always public. Ombiasa prescribe medicine but may also advise offerings and impose fady (taboo). Tromba prescribe medicine and advise courses of action, but do not prescribe offerings or impose fady. The powers of the ombiasa are located in the sikidy (divination) and specialized medical knowledge, but the powers of the tromba are located in the spirits of the dead kings who appear through the body of the tromba. In both cases such power is completed only by the knowing participation of the client/patient.

When illnesses were cured by the initial "private" treatment and when favorable outcomes gave evidence of a harmonious relation between the individual and the supernatural, all actions, thoughts, and utterances involved might be termed *conjunctive,* following Beattie's terminology (Beattie 1970:40). The circle of relations between natural and supernatural was not broken. But when matters did not go well, when cures failed to take effect, or when the promise of a sacrifice seemed not to be recognized, the circle was widened because an outside specialist, the ombiasa/mpisikidy, was consulted, and a more powerful ritual officiant made offerings *on behalf of* the individual, using wider, specialized knowledge and techniques. Or the tromba was consulted and the individual's problems were made public (tromba performed in front of an audience) as well as being referred to a foreign realm of the supernatural, the realm of Sakalava dynasties—who, it was hoped, could exert power over the Tsimihety ancestral and spiritual realm.

There were regular undertakings and events in life that, while not necessarily dangerous in and of themselves, needed to be properly done, not only in the correct way but also at the right time. This included building a house, getting married, taking a long journey, moving to live elsewhere, looking for cattle, complying with requests, and so forth. As well as being subject to spiritual influences, such enterprises were also subject to astrological influences (*vintana*), or rather these life events were *part* of the supernatural. They were not initiated until the propitious time and course of action had been determined by the mpisikidy, who consulted the sikidy in the presence of his client, or clients where groups such as fianakaviana or whole villages were involved. The power of prediction entailed was thought to be in the sikidy itself rather than in the one who set out the seeds. The mpisikidy stressed that it was the seeds speaking, not him. Such divinations were often public (compared to the private consultation of the sikidy made by the ombiasa) but the mpisikidy, like the tromba, was a connector between disparate fragments of complex events. As interpreter of the sikidy, which specified the vintana, the mpisikidy was a connecting functionary.

The principal threats to the cherished freedom of Tsimihety, outside of foreign invaders, were the powers responsible for illness, failure, bad luck, and destiny. The management of these threats involved the employment of specialists, the ombiasa, the mpisikidy (these two were often the same), the tromba, and the mpijoro. Did the association of these specialists with dangerous powers make them powerful people to the extent that they occupied superior positions which gave them political authority within Tsimihety life? Did their dominant position as consultants accepting clients establish within Tsimihety life a hierarchy?

Ombiasa

Among Tsimihety of Androna the term *ombiasa* subsumed three specialized roles: *mpisikidy,* the interpreter of the sikidy when used to diagnose causes of illness and bad luck; *mpanandro,* the interpreter of the sikidy when used to map out a person's horoscope and its bearing on proposed undertakings; and *ombiasa* or healer. In some cases these three roles were taken by quite separate people, but in and around the villages of Androna they were usually one and the same.

Sikidy was a Malagasy-wide divination system of Arabic origin. It was based on sixteen arrangements of seeds that were "read" according to various conjunctions, order of appearance, and the overall tableaux they formed. The arrangements could be read horizontally, vertically, and diagonally. Each figure in the sikidy also had a corresponding astrological association so that sikidy could be used for horoscopes; conversely, the horoscope of an individual gave him or her a particular identity that linked back with the sikidy. There was no doubt of the complexity of the mechanics of the sikidy, and it required considerable training and education. Added to this was the more subtle, less rulebound talent for interpreting, for "seeing" what the sikidy might be saying.

Ombiasa had to be taught sikidy, and sometimes they learned from a father, which made the sikidy an "inherited" skill. But, as often, an ombiasa, realizing he was getting old and his powers were on the wane, might choose his successor and tell him all he knew. On other occasions an ombiasa might call for his "heir," clasp his hands, and pass on his

Fig. 2. Sikidy figures

powers. Younger men—and ombiasa were always men—felt the calling and sought to apprentice themselves to admired ombiasa. Apprentices paid for their education by contributing labor to a man's fields, by paying measures of rice, and by presenting a young heifer. Money was also acceptable. Becoming an ombiasa was open to all men; remaining an ombiasa depended on continuing success as a diviner, consultant, and healer. There was then a competitive market. In some villages there may have been as many as four or five ombiasa, and in other villages there were none. The free market led to specialization, particularly in healing. Some specialized in mending broken bones, some in childhood growth and illness, some in advising on the building up of herds, some on the locating of lost or stolen animals, some in a sort of psychiatric counselling, being known for their good advice and their ability to help people with psychological problems. Ombiasa charged a fee for their services: up to 500 Malagasy francs when a protracted sikidy consultation was involved; 5 francs (1 ariary) for a medical consultation, plus a gift of money or rice for a medicine; and another gift of rice, chicken, or even a cow when the patient was cured. They were, as far as I could ascertain, the only Tsimihety who handled money within the specifically Tsimihety economy on a regular and unquestioned basis.

Ombiasa possessed expert knowledge of sikidy, and specialist

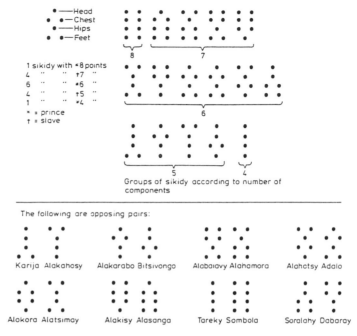

Fig. 3. Sikidy configurations

knowledge of herbs and plants useful for medicines. They were also especially knowledgeable about *fombandrazana* or customs and observances
associated with the foko. This included the different fady of each foko and
also fady that were special to smaller family groups. As part of their
recommended cures, ombiasa prescribed the observance of new fady to
patients and their families. Sometimes, if the patient recovered from a
serious illness, the fady that formed part of the cure were enshrined and
became fady observed by descendants, i.e., new traditions. Like most
adults, ombiasa were sensitive to social and personal relations in their
vicinity. Possessing such different forms of knowledge earned the respect
of client Tsimihety, who at the same time *expected* this. But it also
pushed ombiasa toward a conservatism. They preferred and preserved
traditional medicine because European medicine was beyond their control
and outside their knowledge. Ombiasa frequently recommended the
avoidance of Western goods, foods, and medicines as part of a prescribed
cure, or they diagnosed the cause of illness or bad luck as being a harmful
contact with things, or people, European or "evolué." This included
other, sophisticated Malagasy—Merina in particular. Working for out-

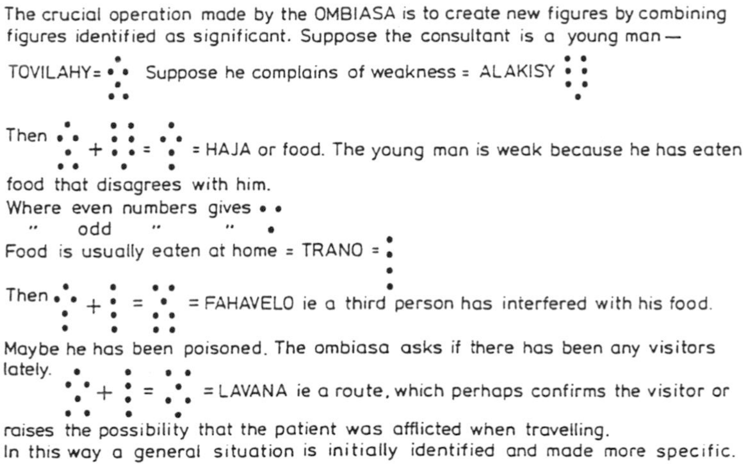

The crucial operation made by the OMBIASA is to create new figures by combining figures identified as significant. Suppose the consultant is a young man —

TOVILAHY = •• Suppose he complains of weakness = ALAKISY ••

Then •• + ••• = •• = HAJA or food. The young man is weak because he has eaten food that disagrees with him.

Where even numbers gives • •
"   odd   "   "   •

Food is usually eaten at home = TRANO = •

Then •• + • = •• = FAHAVELO ie a third person has interfered with his food.

Maybe he has been poisoned. The ombiasa asks if there has been any visitors lately.

•• + • = ••• = LAVANA ie a route, which perhaps confirms the visitor or raises the possibility that the patient was afflicted when travelling.

In this way a general situation is initially identified and made more specific.

Fig. 4. Preliminary manipulation of Sikidy

siders, or on nontraditional projects, such as road building or the construction of schools, might also be divined as a cause of misfortune and lead to ombiasa imposing fady on individuals and their families. In this way, ombiasa not only were a conservative force, they were also a creative and renewing force of fomba Tsimihety, the Tsimihety tradition. It is possible that in this way ombiasa encouraged and buttressed the passive resistance to the outside that was manifest in the failure of individuals to turn up to work on the roads, or keep appointments even when they had agreed to do so. When confronted with their broken promises people explained about the fady, and the displeasure of the ancestors. This was observed by administrators (often in writing in their reports) as being evidence of the individualism and stubbornness of Tsimihety and therefore as the great impediment to modernization. From the Tsimihety point of view, then, it could be argued that the conservatism of the ombiasa was as much a means of resistance, of leadership from behind and underground. Had I understood this I would have inquired further. For example, I do not know whether there was ever any formal prohibition against ombiasa, which would have indicated an awareness of the political role of the ombiasa. But I do find references in my notes to administrators (the sous prefet) and the doctor fulminating against ombiasa.

When ombiasa acted as mpisikidy, especially when they consulted the tableaux to determine the timetables of undertakings such as weddings, house building, if and when to abandon a village, journeys, when

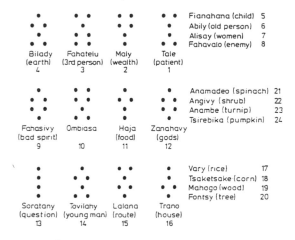

Fig. 5. Layout of Sikidy consultation

to begin the harvest, or when and whether to open a new tomb, they exercised a direct political control on individuals and on collectivities. In their advice they could actually initiate such actions or forestall them even though in matters such as the shifting or opening of tombs their advice was not sufficient and their authority not necessary. Such decisions were necessarily matters for the rayamandreny or elders of the foko concerned. From the point of view of domestic politics the knowledge possessed by the ombiasa of the state of relations among locals was possibly the most significant. Through his authority to diagnose and prescribe, the ombiasa could manipulate relations, repairing bad ones, or upsetting others. Tsimihety people spent much time journeying and visiting and when they did they exchanged news of happenings and relations. Ombiasa, most often older men, had even more time than middle-aged or younger parents to visit around and keep up with what was happening in different places. When visitors came to a village, ombiasa learned from them as well. It was not only that ombiasa could use this knowledge in the privacy of consultations, they used this privately acquired knowledge in their more public capacity as village or faritany elders when the population met to discuss public issues (fokon'olona).

The classic institution cited in ethnographic studies by which political power is covertly managed is witchcraft. Among the Sakalava the divinations of the ombiasa inevitably lead to the identification of witchcraft (Gardenier 1986). And this, in turn, is a mainspring for mobility. But though witches (*mpamosavy*) were recognized by Tsimihety, they were

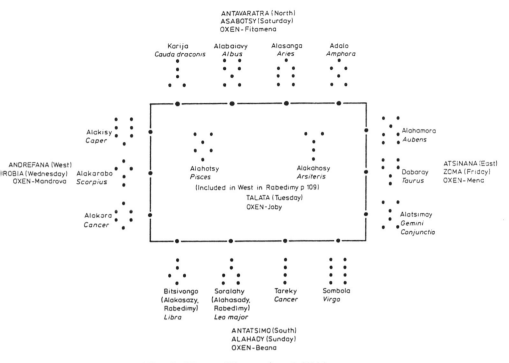

Fig. 6. House, Vintana, and Sikidy

rarely, if ever, identified by ombiasa as the causes of misfortune. Witches were eccentric old women, for the most part, who wandered around the village at night. Spirits (*kalanoro*) also came out at night, so these women ran the danger of being associated with such spirits. But so far as I could make out I did not find witchcraft a significant power in Tsimihety life. Ombiasa identified a variety of mischievous, or wicked, spirits (kalanoro, *zanambatrotraka, zanahary*) to be the causes of mishaps and misfortunes. In addition perturbed or dissatisfied ancestors might be identified as the other supernatural source of disturbance. There were, however, reasons for displeasure or for spiritual activity, and these pointed back to neighborly relations, fulfillment (or lack thereof) of kinship obligations and reciprocities, and neglect of ancestors, especially the recently dead, not necessarily by the sick person but by someone associated with him or her. There was no sikidy figure for witchcraft, but significantly there was for the ombiasa himself. If there was anyone with the knowledge and theoretical power to inflict harm by acting at a distance, it was the ombiasa. Divinations could implicate ombiasa, and one mpsikidy could be called upon to cross-check another. The biggest fear that Tsimihety had was a fear of being poisoned, not necessarily fatally but sufficiently to cause discomfort. Stomach upsets, nausea, headaches, bowel disorders, and depressions could all be blamed on poisoning. Knowledge of poisons was fairly widespread, but I am not so sure that too many people actually knew how to prepare them. The one undoubted expert would have to be the ombiasa, and there was no backwardness in admitting this to have been the case.

Ombiasa were combination doctors, advisors, consultants, counsellors, and planning assistants. They were consulted in private but they were publicly known for who they were. As ombiasa they had no political status: they had no decision-making powers, no authority to order people to do one thing and not another, no powers to organize work groups or convene meetings. But they could to some extent control people's actions and conformities incidentally by instructing them to do, or not to do, as part of a cure or as part of the means of achieving their private goals. The general tenor of their advice and cures was such as to insist on "traditional" Tsimihety ways, which not only conserved the sense of Tsimihety as different from others, but also firmed up the opposition of Tsimihety to non-Tsimihety ideas and people. The knowledge of people's affairs and states of mind that the ombiasa gained in the course of functioning as an ombiasa could be put to use when he or she assumed a role as an elder of the village, or in the faritany, or in the fokon'olona, which represented the local administrative divisions (quartier or canton) of central government. But while this informed opinion, it did not invest that opinion with status or rank. The position of ombiasa had no identity among elders and gave a man no precedence or priority. In his professional capacity the ombiasa had authority by virtue of the knowledge he possessed or was the vehicle of, but ombiasa were to some extent competitive; thus, since patients and clients could vote with their feet, that authority was always socially conditional. Consultations were between social equals. I could find no evidence of ombiasa ever getting together in some form of association and exercising some sort of professional or political clout in this way. Ombiasa were not organized as, for example, tromba sometimes were.

Tromba

It has been argued by some writers that the Malagasy, and in particular the Merina, have a deep-seated psychological need for a benevolent, paternalistic hierarchy. Mannoni argued that the welcoming reception given to European conquerors by the Merina could be accounted for by saying the Europeans met this need. The Europeans, in their turn, had a psychology that, based on their inability to accept a childlike position of dependency in their own societies, made them well-suited to benevolent paternalism (Mannoni 1956). A modification of this thesis about the dependency of the Malagasy on paternal authority was argued by Althabe in trying to describe and explain the situation of the Betsimisaraka immediately after independence. When the French withdrew they left an authority gap that created a crisis in village structure. This could not be filled by reviving a precolonial political system so, according to Althabe, this crisis was overcome by reviving and asserting the tromba (Althabe 1969:117). Unfortunately for Althabe's ground condition, the evidence seems to suggest that Betsimisaraka never did have a well-developed dynastic hierarchy but a weak grouping of local chiefdoms. Many Betsimisaraka, far from welcoming a strong political authority, fled from Merina hegemony and settled in Androna. Nevertheless Althabe's construction of Betsimisaraka postcolonial politics is of interest and has bearing on Tsimihety politics. Tromba were people who, when in trance, were taken over by the regal personages of Sakalava mpanjaka, kings whose rule continued from their inaccessible royal burial places.

These kings, through their mediums, issued orders and recommendations to be followed by Betsimisaraka villagers. Yet, being but spirits, the kings were not "real" and so were beyond the reach of on-the-ground government embodied in police, officials, and functionaries. Being Sakalava, the mpanjakas were not Betsimisaraka, but outsiders with a paternal interest in the welfare of Betsimisaraka. But since the agents, the tromba themselves, were actually living Betsimisaraka, Althabe argues, it turns out that the Betsimisaraka by this devious route actually ran their own affairs in the face of government by the central bureaucracy:

> Ils choississent des maîtres étrangers qui sont leur création ils realisent avec eux une relation de subordination dans laquelle ils jouent le rôle d'intermediaires obligatoires. (Althabe 1969:118)

I do not wish to comment on the details of Althabe's thesis or, for that matter, on whether or not his argument is convincing as a descriptive ethnography or as a model of what goes on. What concerns me is the general observation that Althabe seems to have been led to his complex argument by the perception or intuition that "peripheral" Malagasy (those living off the plateau in contrast to the plateau-living Merina in particular) have to be thought about in the context of the history of political relations—going back to the expansion of the Merina state and including the colonial conquest by the French and subsequent national independence. What marked the Betsimisaraka was the form of their resistance to, and acceptance of, this history of outside intrusion and domination. The relation to domination was many-levelled among the Betsimisaraka, but whereas the surface was deceiving, the "real" relation was the covert one in which real obedience was given to an "imaginary" authority. (This is Althabe's term, and it is arguable whether the tromba and the mpanjaka are imaginary, in the same sense of unreal, as Althabe thinks.)

There was a similar disguised relationship between Sakalava and external authority, again probably originating from the time of the Merina expansion. Feeley-Harnik, writing of the Sakalava of Analalava, bordering quite close to Tsimihety, describes the condition succinctly:

> Almost 90 years after the French colonized Madagascar, and almost 25 years after independence, the Sakalava of the northwest coast continue to work for the dead kings and queens who once governed them, while participating only marginally in national political economy. . . . Using their own "politics of habitation," they protected their values by "hiding" them in the now illicit realm of the dead, the one place where the natives could not be seized and detained, except by their own means and for their own purposes. (1984:1, 12)

The Sakalava achieved and perpetuated their own political autonomy through ritual, especially through the ritual of the "royal work" and through tromba. But tromba, as vehicles of the dead mpanjaka, were not alien authorities but Sakalava ones. If for the Betsimisaraka they were surrogate external powers, for the Sakalava they were integral and affirmed independence. Betsimisaraka achieved their autonomy indirectly via tromba, and Sakalava maintained their independence directly via tromba. But both peoples maintained an independence that did not involve them in open and defiant opposition, in active resistance and violence. And they did it by erecting a political hierarchy that was private and impervious to bullets, laws and proclamations, and the efforts of formally constituted political authorities.

Tsimihety live between Sakalava and Betsimisaraka and their history was tangled up with both neighbors—and with first Merina, then French conquest, and finally, with the central national government. For these reasons alone it would seem reasonable to suppose that there might be something in common in their reactions to these outside conditions, or even that there was a relation between their reactions. But given some crucial differences between the three cultures, the relationship may be one of variations on a theme. The first important difference was that both Sakalava of the northwest and Betsimisaraka of the northeast were fairly sedentary and inhabited areas in which they had been long settled. Tsimihety were mobile, seminomadic even, and knew themselves to be immigrants. The second important difference was that the Sakalava had a well-developed, long-established political hierarchy that had a ritual as well as a secular base. Betsimisaraka probably never had anything like the dynastic hierarchies of the Sakalava, but a system of local chiefs presiding, often precariously, over loosely aggregated villages. The Tsimihety seemed to have had a political hierarchy that was originally more like that of the Betsimisaraka, though with some tinge of Sakalava admixture. For reasons that are ill-defined, but which have been discussed in chapter 2, such hierarchy as was institutional was dissolved or was never rebuilt after assaults. In 1963, though there were such rank terms as mpanjaka used in certain contexts, Tsimihety appeared to acknowledge no formal or open political hierarchy. But in the light of studies made of Tsimihety neighbors we have to ask whether or not there might have been a hidden political system that not only ordered Tsimihety life and maintained political cohesion, but also directed in some way their resistance to outside domination. In different ways, the tromba was a key figure in the alternative or underground politics of both the Betsimisaraka and the Sakalava, and since tromba feature in Tsimihety life, the question of their possible political significance must be asked.

Tromba were widespread among Tsimihety with at least one present in a small village and its satellite hamlets and several in larger villages. All the tromba I met or saw were women. Most tromba lived as ordinary village people, but some, older women, as far as I could make out, lived alone in small, old-fashioned wood and thatch huts. I was told by everyone with whom I raised the subject that, soon after the rebellion of 1947, during the early 1950s, there were a large number of tromba who were organized into "chapters," each chapter recognizing an order of seniority among its members that was based, in part, on the relative power and prestige of the dead rulers who possessed the tromba, and in part on the seniority of a person as the actual tromba. The administrative records of the time speak of a tromba "cult" and "outbreaks" of tromba. Administrators advised they were keeping a close watch in case anything dangerous should develop. From the lack of further comment I conclude nothing did develop. Some Tsimihety told me, with great amusement, about the days when there would be thirty or more tromba all in trance at the same time. Nevertheless I did detect remnants of tromba organization in 1963. I was present at one séance in which seven tromba participated, and six of them deferred to the seventh. The joint session had clearly been organized beforehand.

Unlike Betsimisaraka, Tsimihety tromba conducted trance sessions in their own homes in the village and not in specially constructed huts out in the rice fields. For the séance the floor space was clearly divided between a "stage" (which was in some cases a raised platform) and the auditorium. On some occasions this division was marked by curtains. For most of the time the tromba remained on the stage, though she/he did go among the audience. The tromba had two or more assistants (*rajao*), one who played a drum and a second who helped the tromba into trance and assisted her/him in dressing in the royal robes. Additional assistants played the accordion and assisted in dressing and preparations.

Tsimihety séances were similar to those described by Althabe. On stage was a small table and a white cloth with a plate or shallow bowl of water containing a coin; next to this was a china plate with white earth and a cup (*fanimbohana*) containing incense (*emboka*). As the drum and/or accordion played a monotonous descending three-beat rhythm, the tromba worked herself into trance with the assistant(s) helping by holding her by the shoulders as she shook and then dressing her in the red robes of the mpanjaka (*lamba mena*) over a white shirt. She wore a broad-brimmed straw or raphia hat, carried a white towel in one hand, and staff of office in the other (kiboay). Once in trance and dressed "she" became "he." The voice changed into a man's voice, he often smoked a cigarette (Tsimihety women rarely, if ever, smoke), and he began to stride imperiously about the stage. He offered cigarettes to members of the audience (these were usually refused). Often he talked in tongues that claimed to be Arabic, Hindi, or Persian. I could not verify any of these claims. The tromba went among the audience with the white earth and daubed people on the forehead, saying that he could see they were getting ill and this would prevent the illness. The speeches were often long, but were interrupted by asides and comments in Malagasy—as when, for example, I, the vazaha, was welcomed. On another occasion, comments were made by the tromba on the village slackness in keeping vermin away from the rice fields.

Tromba séances were frequently arranged to treat ailments and illnesses that had not yielded to other treatments. The patient requested a séance ahead of time and the patient(s) was then addressed directly by the tromba during the speeches. The tromba came directly to the patient, announcing he sensed illness. He questioned the patient and, if it was a child, for example, he took it in his arms, daubed white clay on the forehead or affected part, whispered words, and prescribed a medicine, which on every occasion I attended included a prescription for aspirin as well as a traditional recipe. At some point the tromba sprayed eau de cologne over the audience, or, dipping the ends of the toga in the water, sprinkled it over the audience. (This is an echo of the Malagasy form of blessing, *tsodrano,* whereby water that has been in contact with the sacred figure is sprayed over a congregation.) Sometimes tromba asked if there was anyone else sick who needed curing. Sometimes, as I have said, they identified as ill people who did not know they were. Séances often went on through the night, but after five or six hours they seemed to peter out. With the aid of the assistants the tromba came out of trance and, apparently, remembered nothing. The next day she resumed normal daily life.

At this point I must make a short personal aside. At the time tromba struck me as the most exotic "anthropological" feature of Tsimihety I had witnessed. Possession trance was, and still is to me, strange not just to my own life experience but to my own sympathy. Only people quite "different" from me could go into trance. I was all the more thrown by the fact that Tsimihety, far from regarding tromba and possession as something powerful and extraordinary, treated tromba with a degree of lightheartedness and skepticism. As far as most people present at a séance were concerned, they were there for the entertainment and certainly not for any serious political or ritual motives. A séance had all the makings of sacred drama—incense, a crowded room, a tense performer becoming possessed and undergoing a transformation before one's very eyes. And hypnotic music. But people came and went, providing they could get through the crowd; not everyone took notice of the tromba all the time. Young men, in particular, came in and out of the back of the room, or stayed outside the doorway and shouted in mild obscenities, impertinent questions, and derisive comments. If the remarks were funny, everyone laughed, except the tromba who either ignored them or fired back angry replies, sometimes with considerable wit and sarcasm. Men, in particular, would make pointed remarks about the transvesticism of the tromba, implying homosexuality on the part of the woman. (During the day when visiting villages Tsimanefa, my assistant, would sometimes remark of a woman that she was lesbian and also tromba.) Men asked for news about life on Nossi Bé, the island where the kings possessing the tromba originated, news of the weather, of how the women there were behaving, and whether the reason the king had come to the village that evening was because the women were giving the mpanjaka a hard time. Women, especially those with young children present, tended to be more attentive to the tromba, as did the older women, but they were not slow to laugh or to converse among themselves, a sure sign that the tromba was not claiming all their attention. It would be tempting to consider the tromba as dramatizations of the relations between the sexes, a symbol of domestic politics, since tromba were predominantly women who became men and took over political positions. I lack the information to pursue this possibility or to refute it entirely. I do, however, prefer to think of tromba as the most aesthetically developed form of Tsimihety entertainment that took place on a regular basis rather than as a serious politico-ritual event. If the tromba took herself seriously, most of the audience certainly did not, and she was very much like an actor whose job was to act properly for the entertainment of others—not like the ombiasa whose job was not to *act* with a patient, whose job it was to be seriously ill. There might be a serious patient at a séance, but he or she was part of the performance for the audience. Tromba were much like the boxers at a *moraingy.* While the two young men were in the center of the circle of spectators they fought seriously for the entertainment of others, but it was not a "serious" fight because of friction between them. Their fight was entertainment, and so was tromba, even when members of the audience went into trance as well. If there was political significance to the tromba it was that the concept of mpanjaka was a thing of the past—so far removed from present-day realities as to be seen as a theatrical figure. Some Tsimihety did perform plays and these featured mpanjaka, but I never watched any and have no other information. Mpanjaka were institutions other people had, such as the Sakalava. In actual fact, in the village of Maringibato, on the western edge of Androna, there were people who called themselves Zafinifotsy and who were spoken of as mpanjaka. Their appearance was certainly different from Tsimihety since some of the old men wore red greatcoats and the older women went bare-breasted. But these people were looked upon as curiosities, survivors from the past. Even so, they were reputed to possess effective rain rituals that they carried out on request for Tsimihety.

Unless mpanjaka gave political advice via tromba regarding what to do about political problems and I never caught any political nuances in their performance, I do not think that tromba were political figures, as they were in Betsimisaraka, or politico-ritual figures, as they seemed to be in Sakalava. In the 1950s they may well have served political functions as a focus for protest and underground resistance, perhaps as reaction to the traumatic events of 1949, but by the time of my study they were no more than imitators and entertainers.

Mpijoro and Soja

Joro was the general term for prayer, offering, or sacrifice, and anyone offering publicly was *mpijoro*. But it also specified a "natural" office— that occupied by the senior person (preferably male) of the senior generation of whatever association might be involved. A man, as head of the household, might casually sprinkle rum, or any liquid, on the ground and ask the ancestors to assist him, or not to interfere with the day. As he poured the liquid he was mpijoro. But on the occasion of an illness, say, or if he wished to make a serious promise (*manalatsikafara*) that he would sacrifice an ox to the ancestors when his enterprise had succeeded, he would call upon the senior male of the senior generation of the fianakaviana, specifically ambenilahy, to make the promise and the later offering on his behalf in front of all the kinsfolk. In matters that concerned the village, such as the opening of the season, the harvest, and troubles that seemed to affect everyone (vermin, bad weather), the offering to the ancestors was made by the mpijoro of the zafintany. Sometimes a vahiny living in a village would ask the mpijoro of the zafintany to offer for him. When ancestors and spirits had to be addressed on matters concerning death, famadihana, and the tomb, the mpijoro was the senior member of the senior generation of those of the foko present for the occasion. (I was never quite clear whether, on the occasion of a burial, the mpijoro was in fact the senior male of the mpiambinzana, the trustees, or the senior member present, whether mpiambinzana or not.)

The duty of the mpijoro was to speak to the ancestors. First they were invoked either as an anonymous collectivity, or by running through an abbreviated genealogy that began from the mpijoro and worked up to an original ancestor, the one who first settled in Androna. On certain occasions, though, a specific ancestral spirit was called upon by name if it was thought to be personally responsible for causing the upset. (This knowledge was inferred, often with the assistance of the ombiasa, from a reconstruction of past relations of omission and commission. For example, after persistent illness it was decided that an infant who had not been given his first heifer was restless and frustrated and was causing the illness.) If an animal was to be killed, the mpijoro supervised the killing, ensuring the proper orientation of the animal, the catching of the blood, and the butchering. While it was killed the mpijoro recited the names of the ancestors. Then he superintended distribution of the meat to ancestors—who got the offal, including the intestines that had been specially washed by children—and to his kin, which included the immediate kin of the supplicant. Finally, seated before the severed head of the beast, the mpijoro again named ancestors either in sequence or collectively and stated the point of the offering in a very matter-of-fact voice:

> Here is your cow, your part given by the whole family. Stay peaceful in the tomb. Ask no more of the living. Here is your part. We are gathering here to give a cow to the dead (name). The cow belongs to _____ , father of the deceased. We thank those here for coming.

The mpijoro then washed his hands in a bowl of water and sprinkled the congregation, beginning with the children—the traditional mode of blessing. Everyone was then invited to eat the meat and rice, which the young men had cooked.

No one man, or one descent line, possessed the office of mpijoro and could be said thereby to be set apart, or above others. There was no monopoly of ritual power by some people. If there was a specialization of control of ritual power it was part of the general precedence of seniority and gender. This was based on the supposition that those who were senior were in closer touch with the ancestors. But this was only a special case of the general differentiation and respect accorded to age and seniority. It was a pervasive principle that priority and precedence were accorded to the senior person or group in any situation. In collective situations precedence was given to the zafintany, who were by definition senior, and in interpersonal situations precedence was given to the senior male of the senior generation (who may not be the eldest person present). Anyone could be mpijoro depending on the situation and who was present.

The situation was similar to the position of soja, which meant master or head. I heard the term most frequently used to designate the heads of the constituent fizarana or sections in a village, while the soja of the zafintany was the sojabe, the senior headman. His house was known as the *tranamponga,* the house where the drum was kept to summon village meetings (kabary or fokon'olona). The sojabe often chaired the meeting but, other than the fact that he was always accorded polite respect, I did not notice that he carried any more weight because he was sojabe. The principle of seniority applied when an entire faritany, including its component villages, became involved. And such officiating at welcomes or offerings was made by the soja of that village regarded as the chief village in ritual terms. The term used to describe the status of all senior members was *tompoko.* Everyone who belonged to the zafintany in a district was tompontanana, or a senior member, by virtue of original ancestral settlement and the presence there of their tombs. Tompoko was also used to describe an individual owner of cattle or other property, and was the term of politeness used to greet anyone (*salaama tompoko!*). Soja, then, was a term that appeared to denote political responsibility without having attached to it any political rights; in this sense, it was the secular counterpart of the ritual office of mpijoro, who also had only responsibilities and no rights.

Seniority and Gender

It was clear that the hierarchical offices of mpijoro and soja were not exclusive statuses. They were special, well-defined, particular instances of the general precedence accorded to seniority and to males. In the kinship terminology, kin of the same generation who were similarly designated were differentiated by seniority (*zoky,* elder; *zandry,* younger), and this was extended to the issue of an elder sibling, who was senior to the offspring of a younger sibling. Less formally, but more evident in everyday life, was the respect accorded to the elderly, to whom one deferred on matters concerned with fomba or tradition. I was often referred to older men for answers to my questions, even though the person I asked knew the answer; and this was even more true when, as it transpired, one man was simultaneously sojabe, mpijoro, and ombiasa. Politically the old men of a village, or any population that assembled together to discuss public affairs, were respectfully identified and treated as *rayamandreny,* the mothers and fathers. In the public meeting (fokon'- olona, or kabary) attended by all inhabitants, the rayamandreny sat together and controlled the meeting. Rayamandreny tried to bend the meeting one way or another, or articulate and summarize the gist of opinions until the sojabe, as the last to speak, summed up and presented a consensus that was also a final opinion. But though everyone, not just rayamandreny, tried to manipulate discussion, I have no evidence that the sojabe had any power of office to sway things, let alone give orders and enforce sanctions.

The privilege of age and seniority was part and parcel of the direction of life itself, an ascent toward ancestorship that was an ascent toward the assumption of "real," albeit supernatural, power. Parallel to this vertical dimension in Tsimihety life was the clear precedence of the male over the female sex. In daily life, this was instanced whenever male and female walked together—male first, female behind, children last; male empty or light-handed, female with burden. When formally entertaining visitors to a meal, males ate separately in the main hut where the meal was put deferentially before them. The female entered crouching and left crouching and backwards. Some women tasted the food first in sight of the guests. Women ate together in the kitchen. The rayamandreny did not, officially, include women, but when everyone was assembled, the women gathered together nearby and talked loudly among themselves, offering their opinions. Similarly, on ordinary everyday occasions men and women ate together quite often and quite informally, and the seemingly abject inferiority of women was quite discarded. For some villages I have notes which indicate that a woman was regarded as mpijoro because she was the senior member of the senior generation of the zafintany, but I could get no agreement among people that this would apply as a general principle, i.e. that if there was no appropriate senior male, a female could assume ritual duties. But nowhere did I find a woman who was soja. Although there were all the formal signs of a hierarchy of men over women, the relations between men and women were far more the relations between equals. Men and women often sat around the hearth during the day talking and snacking on roast corn. But just as often men sat in small groups and women sat separately in their small groups. For much of the day men and women maintained separate lives, though how separate depended largely on age: older men and women sat around often talking together, while those engaged in subsistence tasks went their own ways according to the division of labor. But in the preparation of rice fields, at harvest and during growth of the crop when people often lived in the rice fields, men and women did separate tasks alongside each other, keeping up a constant banter. Large-scale public meals saw the sexes eating separately, but at daily private meals they often ate together with children. This paralleled the fact that on public occasions men did the cooking and on private domestic occasions cooking was the woman's work. Women did control the granaries and if a man wanted rice for any purpose, to offer a guest or to sell, he asked the woman for it.

Chef de Village: Chef de Quartier

This chapter would not be complete without mention of these local officials, though their relevance to the issues under discussion is minimal (albeit increasing). The independent Malagasy administration followed the French approach by considering as a village what Tsimihety considered to be many villages or hamlets. Each village nominated a man as "chef," and this appointment was confirmed by the sous prefet in Mandritsara. One of these village chiefs was deputed head of a quartier; there were four quartier in a canton. These local officials were paid by the central administration; their responsibilities included communicating government directives to villagers, organizing road corvée, and assisting in collecting taxes and in census taking of both people and cattle. On the other side these officials were spokesmen for the villagers to the administration, and they delivered the village opinion. Inasmuch as central government agencies at the district level had very definite powers, it would be wrong to deny that chefs had access to power and hence had authority in the villages and in the course of daily life. However, Tsimihety were dead-set against fanjakana or officials and outside government, and chefs nominated by the villagers themselves through confirmation by the administration were invariably men who could be trusted to be on the Tsimihety side.

Insofar as it is permissible to generalize, it would be true to say that chefs were agents of the village rather than the government. Villagers looked to their chefs to come and go between them and the government—to explain, for example, why people could not turn up for road working, why neither rice, cash, nor cattle were available to meet tax requirements. At the same time, when chefs returned from their meetings in Mandritsara they relayed the intentions of the administration as well as its orders. By their contacts with central government, chefs got to learn of the presence in Mandritsara of, e.g., agricultural officials or health officials intending to "inspect" or to begin the process of some new development. Even more threatening, the movements of the gendarmerie were reported. The point is that with this intimation of possible future activity, villagers could take evasive action in good time.

The men nominated by villagers to be chefs were often younger and could speak and read some French and could read Malagasy. If a man had been to school, this was often a sufficient qualification, the point being that these were men who best understood the ways of the external, governmental world. They could keep villagers abreast of government goings on and intentions, and advise them on possible courses of action. A village meeting always listened attentively to the chef de village/ quartier. When outsiders came to a village it was always the chef de village who welcomed them, chaperoned them, and assumed the duties of hospitality that would otherwise be undertaken by the soja. It was the job of the chef to shunt the visitor away as quickly as possible and to divert or distract his or her attention from the village and its affairs. Until I became a familiar figure in certain villages in Androna I was always welcomed and shepherded by the chef de village rather than by the soja. Needless to say, this shielding did not make it any easier to obtain reliable information.

The condition that chefs be nominated by villagers was, of course, part of the French colonial policy of ruling through the people themselves. But it assumed that such officials would be loyal to the administration that employed them, rather than to their electorate. In the Tsimihety case the vast majority of chefs were agents of the village rather than the government. But having these responsibilities of representing the village did give the chefs a certain degree of authority in village affairs. They knew best what courses of action to follow to avoid notice by the government, and while they had no power to enforce policies, the force of their opinion was powerful. However, chefs could call in the power of the central administration to control affairs in the village, and this capability was an uneasy presence in the village. I came across only one instance during my stay of the police being summoned by a chef de village to manage village affairs. This was when rice had been stolen from a granary. The village tried in vain to locate the culprit(s). The chef brought in the police when a second granary was broken into and the thieves, two Betsileo from a nearby village, were apprehended.

Far more threatening to Tsimihety than the presence in their midst of agents of central goverment in the persons of chefs was the insidious presence of agents of the ruling Parti Sociale Démocratique (PSD). By the very nature of the situation, I can say very little, but my suspicions were confirmed when President Tsiranana visited Mandritsara during my stay. The situation, in brief, was that the national political situation in Madagascar revolved around the opposition between the traditionally dominant and numerically superior Merina living in the central plateau, together with the Betsileo—and the rest, the peripheral peoples. Tsiranana had led a coalition of peripherals (PSD) to victory over the central Merina Ankotony Kongreiny Fahaleovantenan Madigasikara (A.K.F.M.). But to uphold his position, the president had to sustain his support in the periphery, and nowhere was this more crucial than in his home territory, Androna. For reasons I have already intimated, President Tsiranana (the epitome of outside government, of fanajakana) was regarded with ambivalence by Tsimihety, and enthusiasm for the PSD was, shall we say, diluted. By combinations of bribes, promises, threats, and coercion, a number of individuals had been turned into agents and informers for the PSD. Their job was to whip up enthusiasm in the villages for the PSD and to inform of any opposition. Not only villagers were subject to this surveillance: foreigners, traders, and visitors were subject to such monitoring as having mail checked, phone calls listened in on, financial and trading transactions reported, and movements generally watched. As it happened, during the period of my stay nothing overt or threatening came about. But it is not beyond the bounds of possibility that the reticence of Tsimihety was influenced by the atmosphere of anxiety generated by party politics being insinuated into a village context.

Conclusion

Though I have emphasized Tsimihety egalitarianism and liberty, power was a feature of their lives, and the varieties of power had their particular agents—the ombiasa (understood here as the composite of mpanandro, mpisikidy, and ombiasa); tromba; and the mpijoro/soja. Alien power agents were the chefs de villages/chefs de quartiers, and the unnamed agents of the PSD.

The power of the ombiasa to influence people was entirely individual since he only operated on the basis of individual, private consultation. Ombiasa did not address assemblies in any way as ombiasa (though they may have done so as rayamandreny), so they were not leaders in any overt sense. Ombiasa were volunteer specialists, men who made a deliberate decision to seek knowledge and expertise. They were not "called" to their occupation by some outside "power." Furthermore, the reputation of ombiasa depended on their success ratio absolutely and, in part, on their success relative to other ombiasa. Though not with any intention, ombiasa competed with others in a weak fashion. The power of the ombiasa rested in (1) successful diagnosis of illness, (2) successful prescriptions of medicines and amulets (*ody*), (3) accurate predictions, and (4) convincing warnings about the future. These were all based on sikidy divination. Sikidy gave the horoscope of an individual (vintana), an indication of the future course of events, and whether undertakings would succeed or fail; it also pinpointed the cause of illness, bad luck, failure, injury, and so forth. But though sikidy could be learned as an abstract system, its operation was at no time abstract. Rather it was an integral part of the life and illness of the patient and the doctoring of the ombiasa. The patient's crisis, the reading of the sikidy, the events and personnel nominated by the sikidy, and the actions of the ombiasa were all part and parcel of the same thing—all had the same cause (most commonly to be found among the ancestors). The ombiasa was not, then, a person with power over another so much as he was a person in whose power it rested to complete a series of events that first erupted in crisis (illness) or anxiety (future undertakings). In thise sense, ombiasa, sikidy, and patient/client were equally parts of a singular, but complex form of life. Just as the patient did not know the how and the why of the illness or misfortune, but knew only that it lay somewhere in the vintana, so the ombiasa did not claim as his the knowledge in the sikidy but only that he was the instrument through which the sikidy "spoke." Likewise the medical, herbal knowledge gained by the ombiasa was not different from the medical knowledge acquired by Tsimihety adults and practiced as home remedies. It was an extension of it. There was, however, the character "ombiasa" in the sikidy, which indicated that ombiasa could themselves inflict misfortune. In this sense, since ombiasa had special access to powers, they were to some extent feared, and this gave them an ill-defined position of power in the community.

Tromba, in contrast with ombiasa, were called to their position, in the sense that tromba were women whose mundane identity was periodically dispossessed by the spirit of dead kings, who then possessed their bodies. Tromba, too, may be called into operation by the advent of illness or failure, but they did not have to be. Tromba could perform on their own initiative, or when their ruling mpanjaka desired to make his presence known. But the mpanjaka were not woven into the pattern of Tsimihety life, as perhaps they once were when Sakalava influence was greater; tromba were not part of the one form, as ombiasa, sikidy, illness, and patient were. Mpanjaka were ghosts from a past history long since departed and changed. Yet mpanjaka were also, for present-day Sakalava, contemporary and meaningful. So given these conditions, the tromba could be viewed as entertainment, during which it was possible to ridicule hierarchy in its most extreme form—divine kingship. Sakalava mpanjaka were prime examples of external ranks that could be rendered powerless by incorporating them into a quite alien framework, theater. In contrast, the Betsimisaraka seconded mpanjaka by "inviting" them in as "rulers."

I pointed out that it was men far more than women who made fun of tromba and treated them as theatricals. The tromba herself, and the women in her audience, were undoubtedly moved. It was also the case that neighboring tromba were ranked, but how this affected their interaction, if at all, I cannot say. Clearly there was a difference between men and women in this respect, but other than remark on this I can say no more.

Mpijoro (and soja) were "natural" offices filled by the accident of birth order and based entirely on the principle of seniority. The mpijoro was the spokesman for others, but he said no more than they knew or intended. He was the spokesman for the living to the dead on the occasions of sacrifice and offerings (joro), and during the performance of these representative duties the mpijoro enjoyed a separate status from his kin. But it was not an exclusive office, nor was it hereditary. Filling the role of mpijoro was relative to the definition of the particular assembly—household, extended household, family, section, foko, village, etc. Similarly, the soja was the secular counterpart, the chairman of the particular assembly whose role was based on seniority qualifications.

No power accepted by Tsimihety was based on the possibility of coercion. But power imposed on them through the office of chef and the role of informer was based on coercion. By and large the office of chef had been appropriated functionally by Tsimihety, but not structurally.

But the role of the informer and the pressure of party politics was a threat they had yet to come to terms with.

Tsimihety life was in one sense pervaded by a cocoon of power, the power of the ancestors. But in this they were no different from other Malagasy. Where they differed from many others was that this pervasive power was nowhere expressed in social hierarchies, ranks, and statuses. Nor was it ritually concentrated since the mpijoro was but an agent of his kinfolk who acted on their behalf vis-à-vis the ancestors, but who had absolutely no authority or power derived *from* the ancestors to persuade his kin. The difficulties of everyday life—quarrels, minor thefts, fights (which rarely occurred)—were settled by talking in meetings of the parties concerned either in private, or if necessary, in public before the elders. Other than the authority of the father and the mother over their children, no individuals were empowered to coerce others. It was in illness and misfortune that Tsimihety confronted their own helplessness in the face of invisible powers. To combat these powers they enlisted the aid of the ombiasa so that, in the sense that the ombiasa "had the power" to combat, he had power. In the sense that the ill individual depended on the success of the ombiasa the individual was in the power of the ombiasa. But, as I have shown, this dependence was never total. Other healers could be consulted.

Overall, power in Tsimihety life was at a low level, and possible means for its concentration were weak or lacking. Wealth was temporary and could not form the basis for power: charismatic leaders required their followers, and Tsimihety were too given to moving around and away from anything they perceived as domination. Charismatic and talented individuals trod on stony ground in Androna and tended to leave. While the realities of invisible powers were manifest through illness and misfortune, the possibility that dealing with them by opposing or joining powers might be marshalled into political power was dissipated by the confinement of the ombiasa to private consultations. Real power lay with the ancestors, to whom everyone was equally joined (everyone was a future ancestor), but the hierarchy of the living to the ancestors was never embodied in rank. Instead it led off, through death, into a new dimension of life removed from *realpolitik*.

CHAPTER 6

Conclusion

From an economic, subsistence point of view, Tsimihety were rice cultivators. I do not think Tsimihety themselves would deny this. They knew full well they depended on rice. But growing rice was a necessary occupation, something everyone *had* to do. Keeping cattle was what Tsimihety *chose* to do, and how they raised cattle, what they did with them, was what marked out Tsimihety from non-Tsimihety and what brought people together as Tsimihety. Practically, one might say, Tsimihety were sedentary rice cultivators. Idealistically they were seminomadic pastoralists. This contrast is worth pursuing.

Cultivators are usually sedentary, observe well-defined rules of tenure, and are more likely to be hierarchical; pastoralists are usually nomadic and relatively free of constraining rules of tenure and hierarchy. As an observer I would have to admit, and I think the preceding account backs this up, that Tsimihety conformed more closely to a pastoralist sociopolitical pattern than to one founded on sedentary cultivation. Compare Tsimihety with the following "pastoral-nomad" pattern set out by Walter Goldschmidt.

Flexibility and mobility of residence are necessary so that cattle can be moved according to seasonal/pasture variation. This flexibility may be complemented by a linking structure of patrilineages (which are often associated with aggressive, "masculine" behavior). Cattle themselves are used to bring new social relations into being, e.g. cattle are generally exchanged as part of a bridewealth. In pastoral societies personal and political status is built on the acquisition of cattle (which in turn may call upon military prowess) and on entrepreneurial skill in the cattle "market." Variability in such skills and success leads to variability of ownership status, but this is countered by physical and social mobility and the ever-present opportunities for individuals to achieve status. In pastoral societies ceremonial life tends to be quite meager (but rites of passage are important) and ritual importance is placed on cattle. Covert aggression, as in witchcraft, is unimportant since people are always free to leave. On the other hand, pastoralists are highly dependent on divination and prediction. Goldschmidt concludes his summary by suggesting that pastoralists have a pride, a hauteur, a strong sense of individual worth, and a strong sense of the nobility of pastoralism as a calling. (The foregoing is a summary of Goldschmidt 1979:15–27. I have placed in parentheses traits that did not apply to Tsimihety.)

The pride and hauteur of which Goldschmidt speaks is manifest most openly in the disdain shown by pastoralists for other people, their neighbors, particularly if they are sedentary agriculturalists (e.g., the Nuer "have profound contempt for peoples with few or no cattle, like the Anuak" [Evans-Pritchard 1940:16]). And among neighboring pastoral peoples there is frequently a continuing trial of strength centering on cattle raiding. Is this pride and hauteur part and parcel of the desire to be independent, morally and politically, of others? Coeval with this pride is the sense of independence exhibited by pastoral nomads, who are unwilling to submit to any form of institutionalized political domination, least of all from outside. It might be observed here that "pride and hauteur" toward other groups is close to a form of xenophobia and discrimination on the basis of group membership. Though it lacks the aggressive component, Tsimihety distrust and dislike of outsiders, especially of Merina and Europeans, had a comparable dimension in the desire for independence, a pride in self-sufficiency, and a passive resistance to orders and dictates.

The question then arises as to whether and to what extent Tsimihety pursuit of liberty was a true function of the material circumstances of their existence, as generalizations about pastoral-nomadism would suggest, or whether it was the outcome of historical circumstances and the concatenation of individual wishes, which had appropriated the facilities for freedom and equality that a pastoral outlook implied. In simpler English, how far did practice (praxis) determine ideas? Or how far did ideas determine practice?

Immediately it has to be said that unlike other pastoralists, including those in Madagascar such as the Bara, the Tsimihety did not depend on cattle for subsistence. To repeat, cattle were not slaughtered solely for meat eating but only on ritual occasions, so meat was not a regular item of the diet; cattle were not bought or sold, though they were exchanged and bartered; cattle were valued above all for their aesthetic qualities. Milk was not used by most people, and blood was not consumed at all. Although the raising and herding of cattle was a "productive activity," there was only a relatively small material or subsistence benefit. Whatever may follow from Tsimihety pastoralism, its motivation was not economic and its practice was not subsistence-guided. Tsimihety were not dependent to either a greater or lesser degree on nomadic pastoral activities for their survival in any physiological or dietary sense.

It is characteristic of pastoralists that individuals (or individual households) have equal and open rights to grazing lands: "In both tribal areas (Jie, Turkana) there are the same indigenous conceptions regarding the use of pasturelands. The first principle is that there are no specific pasture rights attached to any individuals or groups of any sort. All pasturage is common to all members of a tribe" (Gulliver 1972:31). Not only did Tsimihety follow this principle, they extended it to agricultural rice lands as well, at least as far as individual and household rights were concerned. People living in a faritany enjoyed equal rights with all others living there to the use of land for cultivation and grazing, but they did not enjoy rights of ongoing tenure. It was as if a first principle of pastoralism had been grafted onto cultivation. Not owning land as an individual mitigated against the development of a sense of ownership of fixed property and the possible sense of security and stability this might produce. On the other hand, though it provided no anchor in land to restrain people from moving, the right to use land more or less ensured a security of subsistence.

Did Tsimihety emphasis on freedom, equality, and independence issue from ecological determinants? Although men in particular were preoccupied in much of their thinking with cattle, they spent far more time cultivating than herding—herding was done by young boys for the most part. Men were very worried when grazing deteriorated. Like other pastoralists, a person's herd was usually distributed over several areas, but when the principal region in the faritany ran short of grass thoughts turned to moving on. A sense of the need for freedom of movement, which was essential to pastoralists, was certainly present among Tsimihety. But was it strong and fundamental enough to become ideologically rationalized into a philosophy of freedom, and consciously used as a policy of covert resistance, especially if cattle raising was not a subsistence activity?

Many informants, speaking in general rather than about their own experiences, maintained that worry about adequate pasture was the main incentive to move. Worry about whether rice fields were adequate was not the prime mover, they said, though it certainly entered into considerations to move. However, in other contexts or in other conversations *particularly involving women,* it was quite apparent that whether there was going to be enough rice was always a problem. Was the granary full enough from the previous harvest to meet this year's needs? Or were sufficient rice fields available for everyone for next year to meet all needs? Or was the soil still fertile enough? Everyday grumbles were not about whether the cattle were getting enough grass but whether a household could meet its needs for rice. Consequently, and contrary to what Tsimihety might have said to me directly, I am of the opinion that the motive or pressure to move came from consideratons about cultivation, all the more so since most Tsimihety did not irrigate. But they actually made or couched the decision to move in terms of a shortage of grazing, i.e., in pastoralist terms.

East African pastoralists and pastoralists of the Middle East and southwestern and eastern Asia are often noted as having been expansionist, especially prior to their often forced incorporation into a state. Given the supposed values of pride, aggression, and manliness said to be associated with pastoralism, such expansion has generally been of a military nature, and to have resulted in a situation of domination. The expansion of Tsimihety, both geographically and demographically, had been phenomenal, even if actual figures are taken with a grain of salt. But such expansion could not, it seems to me, be explained as a pastoralist expansion. Tsimihety were far from warlike or aggressive, and rituals of manhood and manliness were virtually absent. It is quite clear that their expansion in the nineteenth century and early twentieth century was not so much aggressive as an escape from Merina and then French aggression. All indications are that Tsimihety expansion was not organized, nor was it a group or political expansion. It was piecemeal, the movement of individual families, households, and hamlets made for their own reasons, in their own time. But these reasons were not unique— the same reasons happened to Tsimihety because Tsimihety were exposed to the same ecological and political contexts. Another way of emphasizing the point I am trying to make is that whereas pastoral expansion, i.e., expansion as a function of the pastoral condition, is active and predatory, Tsimihety expansion was not moved by pastoralism and was passive. It was a response to aggression. It was a means of resistance. It was as if Tsimihety had used the pastoralist frame of mind as a means to achieve their political end—freedom from outside intrusion—just as they had applied the pastoralist idea of land tenure to cultivation.

Although there were ancestral lands that were clearly located and centered on tombs (tanindrazana), and although there were faintly bounded cultivatable regions (faritany), the relative emptiness of Androna and the northeast central part of Madagascar has meant there were neither geographical nor political impediments to mobility. In any case the dispersal of kin allowed that, even within enclosed areas, people could come and go on the basis of their kinship connections. The actual situation was even more open than this. Any Tsimihety could establish residence anywhere as vahiny. In this sense, while ecology did not "determine" mobility or equality in the sense of economic or material parity, it placed few restrictions on its realization by social and cultural norms of access, tenure, use, and residence. Tsimihety use of Androna enabled the realization of basic human survival needs and granted individuals considerable freedom to choose where they would like to live as producers. Perhaps more incidentally, an absence of political hierarchy allowed individuals full control over the products of their labor (no tribute to chiefs or contributions to royal rituals, hence a resistance to taxation). Mechanisms of cooperation (asareky, tambirô, tanimbary omby) provided a minimal background of cooperation, giving all individuals equal aid in production.

Tsimihety certainly shared many characteristics said to be typical of people whose subsistence is ostensibly based on nomadic pastoralism. Of particular importance in the present context were those emphases on freedom and equality, as well as such specifics as an underemphasis on ritual. But in the case of classical pastoralists the implication of the model is that pastoralism is causal or determines the desire for freedom and equality. If this is indeed so, and such a causal argument is certainly questionable (cf. Asad 1979), then it must also depend on the fact that keeping cattle is economically vital and necessary for subsistence. Now this was not the case for Tsimihety. Cattle contributed only marginally to subsistence and were not part of any trade relationship with sedentarists, peasant or urban. Though they may have loved their cattle dearly, Tsimihety were not driven to that love by what they might have perceived as considerations of survival. If, on the other hand, land for rice fields was to be threatened, Tsimihety would certainly have seen this as endangering their economic survival. Rice was food; cattle were beautiful.

Tsimihety emphasis on freedom and equality was not the outcome of the material conditions of production. If this was the case, is it possible that material practices were built upon ideas of freedom and equality, spurred by motives of resistance? I believe this was so to some extent, and also that ideas of freedom and equality had not arisen as a guiding principle out of serious philosophical deliberations but out of historical conditions, particularly the effect that the actions of some people (Merina and French conquerors) have had on other people (Tsimihety). Tsimihety were not a tribe in any structural or ethnic sense. Tsimihety did not even embrace a congeries of autonomous regional tribes, as the Nuer included such entities as eastern Jikany, western Jikany, Buldok, and so on (cf. Evans-Pritchard 1940:8). At best, Tsimihety was made up of scattered ascent entities focused on their own tombs and linked to each other by individual ties of marriage, resulting kinship, and, in some cases, by a joking relationship. Tsimihety was a term that I have suggested denoted a "set," or, in another sense, as suggested by Jean Buxton for the Mandari, a cultural group (Buxton 1958). But I have intimated in this account that the designation given and accepted of Tsimihety has another dimension than the purely cultural—the sharing of a common accent, of common hair styles, of common performances. Tsimihety were people who had a common attitude toward what we might understand as ethical political problems. This common attitude was not derived from a group mind inculcated with shared symbolized ideas. It derived from the reinforcement by individuals of each others' resentments against outside intrusion and interference. As a process, this resentment and reinforcement originated in the experience by individuals of terror, forcible deprivation, coercion, and frustration under the regime of the Merina. These experiences were repeated for numerous, quite separate, individuals who—some from initiative, some from example—reacted by fleeing. This began in the early 1820s, when there were no Tsimihety. Bringing with them their habits, methods, rules, and beliefs, these early Betsimisaraka refugees had their common experience and their similar reactions to unite them, if not politically, then sympathetically. Such, I suggest, was the minimal basis for and origin of Tsimihety. This was amplified by joining up with the Vohilava who already lived in Androna, and was further strengthened by shared experiences of resistance to the Sakalava and then against the Merina, the French, and, finally, the newly independent republic. For in 1963 it was very difficult for isolated, marginal Tsimihety to understand the difference between an independent central government and a colonial one, especially when most of the laws and governing personnel remained the same.

Under these conditions, and in response to them, individuals developed similar frames of mind about similar priorities. The priority was freedom from intrusion and interference by outsiders, particularly those who by their cruel or oppressive actions showed themselves to be different sorts (foko) of beings to Tsimihety. These others put obstacles in the way of people trying to do things their way, or trying to fulfill wishes they had generated for themselves. The Merina, while undoubtedly Malagasy, were *racially* as well as culturally different from Tsimihety (in European terms, Merina were more Indonesian, Tsimihety more African). Europeans (i.e., French) were even more racially, culturally, and linguistically different. And Tsimihety were "racially" different to Merina as well as to French. Given this priority of "rejection by avoidance" to recognize and obey outside, coercive authority identified in racial (or ethnic) terms, its signification in the term *Tsimihety* is understandable. That Tsimihety became a classificatory term often mistaken for a tribal designation is likely the result of European reactions to hearing the term used in various contexts and mistaking it for a political noun (such an instance is recorded for the Mahafaly by Eggert 1986). However, the important point to be derived from this is that given this ethical priority of freedom and independence, that pattern of life which was to fulfill this priority had to be designed to suit. I am not saying either that a great leader lay down a Tsimihety constitution, or that individuals sat down and rationally planned out a way of life that would secure liberty and ensure it. There is no evidence for this. What I am claiming is that throughout Androna a loose but distinct "system" evolved by trial and error, but grounded in Malagasy culture enshrined in the language. This traditional, cultural framework was inherited by Tsimihety as Malagasy but put to new uses and given new meanings by them as a result of their emerging and changing political context. This was guided by aspirations and values rather than by material circumstances. This "system," which I have tried to describe in previous chapters, set up the *conditions* for freedom as Tsimihety saw it, i.e., as it stopped at the border between Tsimihety and outsiders, namely Merina and French. Thus, immigrants from Betsimisaraka came to Androna with possibly weak and unstable forms of chieftainship and hierarchy. At the western edge they met with relics of a strong form of Sakalava hierarchy and in Androna the indigenous Vohilava seem also to have been governed by chiefs who, if not institutionally strong, could achieve power by force of character. Faced with common incursions by Merina, by the comings and goings of Merina troops, and by a constant if not large-scale influx from the East Coast, local government and administration by hierarchical principles slowly withered to become virtually outlawed then (i.e., 1963) by Tsimihety. Tsimihety priorities were best met by egalitarian procedures of decision making and resource allocation, which in turn were best made in small communities or left to individuals. The emphasis on a pastoral ideology was conducive to the priorities of liberty and equality and had been adopted (whether consciously or not I cannot say) even though the material reality was that Tsimihety depended on cultivated rice for their subsistence.

Madagascar fought one of the earliest wars of independence against a European colonial regime, and the uprising in 1949 was one of the most bloody and brutal of all colonial rebellions. Full independence was not gained until 1960. All I wish to infer from this is that as a whole, and in spite of their internal differences, the people of Madagascar (or their leaders) shared a desire for independence from outside rule, rule by foreigners. This was the highest or most general level at which the desire for liberty operated. But within Madagascar, while all shared the desire to be free of the French, some Malagasy were as desperate to be free of any domination by other Malagasy. In general terms, based on past experience and on numerical superiority, this meant freedom from being dominated by Merina (and the Merina may, presumably, have felt a desire to be free of interference in their affairs by non-Merina). Consequently, Tsimihety did not constitute an isolated case in Madagascar. To cite only their immediate neighbors, the Sakalava stubbornly retained their own hierarchy of royalty and commoners and obeyed only the authority of the dead kings as conveyed through their living representatives. Betsimisaraka followed a covert nighttime authority based on tromba while pretending to obey officials during the day. Sakalava, Betsimisaraka, and Tsimihety all embraced the same ethical and ideological priorities but the actual means by which these were realized differed considerably—all for their own reasons, which only a comparative study might reveal. I would also venture to suggest, however, that it is only by understanding that ideas and desires for freedom are relevant at all levels where people are constrained to identify differences as externality that we can understand not simply colonial wars of liberation but also so-called civil wars, guerrilla wars, wars within national boundaries, and ethnic animosities. It also follows that the desire for liberty and its advocacy need not be uppermost at all political levels. Tsimihety may desire freedom from outside interference by Merina but need have no compulsion to press through such an ideology to obtain the freedom of the individual.

Tsimihety as any sort of entity—ethnic group, set, cultural group, tribe, or whatever name one might choose—did not, in all probability, exist much before 1850, certainly not before 1800. There were Vohilava who were perhaps the first settlers in Androna; there were Betsimisaraka immigrants coming from the east, a few Sakalava coming from the west; and, possibly, some individuals from elsewhere in Madagascar found their way into Androna. What seemed to have coalesced these disparate and independent agents into an identity—Tsimihety—was the military intrusion of the Merina, followed by their attempts to impose their will on these people. Had the Merina come as individuals or households intent only on settling into a daily round, they too might have been living in Androna in numbers alongside other migrants and Vohilava. But their entry as an organized force set in motion reactions by individuals that, while never organized at any political level, created a sense of unity and common identity. Until the threat of military force, people in Androna lived isolated and independent lives, but this autonomy they took for granted. They did not know they were free because there was no threat to freedom. With the advent of conquest, or a military presence, the undefined freedom and autonomy that people had enjoyed was now defined and its limits made clear. Confrontation, even though it was weak, nevertheless created the situation in which Tsimihety (1) became Tsimihety, (2) acted so as to secure their autonomy in face of threat and, (3) utilized and reoriented their institutions toward resistance and freedom as well as maintaining their basic functions. What people were made aware of during the course of outside domination was an autonomy and freedom that they had possessed before, but of which they had then been ignorant.

> Issues of this type seem to arise only when forms of life, and the social patterns that are part of them, after long periods in which they have been taken for granted, are upset and so come to be recognized and become the subject of conscious reflection. (Berlin 1969:xlii).

So, almost inevitably, Tsimihety culture and the values that constituted it were conservative. Tsimihety freedom, including that of the individual, was seen to reside in the conditions of the past, because the past was when the cultural world had not been threatened with denial from an intrusive culture, and when the social world had not been threatened with invasion from external societies. The rejection by most Tsimihety of Christianity, Western education, commercial exchange, bureaucracy, and their insistence on remaining as free as possible to live the same sort of life as their ancestors was less a form of cussed nostalgia and more a means of expressing autonomy, which is to remain continually able to be part creators of their moral world (cf. Raz 1986:154). Inasmuch as the idea of regaining a past of which one was not conscious at the time is at the center of numerous conservative cultural renaissances among indigenous people (American Indian, Maori, Afro-American, for example), I suggest the same explanation applies: conservation, whether of a real or invented predomination era, is the key to regaining lost freedoms. But what is perhaps of greater importance is that this conservation tailors the institutions of social structure to these new needs of freedom. Forms of kinship, exchange, decision making, and ritual, the very stuff of a structural analysis of permanence, became, in the Tsimihety instance at least, the strategic and modifiable means for achieving idealistic goals. And, further, their form and practice in 1963 was itself in constant flux and part of an ongoing *historical* process. The previous chapters have shown in what way Tsimihety wrested a living, dealt with the troubles of life and the mysteries of death, and in general attended to the basics of survival, adaptation, and reproduction. I outlined their economic practices, their political practices, and their ordering of relationships in a kinship idiom. But I am also claiming that, as well as these basic functions, their ways and means of survival and living performed other functions of a more abstract, ideological kind. They contributed to the conditions for the political freedom of all Tsimihety from external political forces, and they provided the conditions for the freedom of individuals within the culture. Ethnographers have not often been concerned with freedom. They have tended to follow the precepts of Durkheim's functionalism and to regard institutions and attendant beliefs as constraints. Other anthropologists of a more materialist persuasion have also perceived only the constraining influences of institutions and their determination by subsistence and production. The societies studied by anthropologists, therefore, come across as being unfree societies, where custom or economy is king, rather than as societies in which institutions provide conditions of personal and political freedom. It may well be the case that such societies are unfree and are in the majority, but there are some, like Tsimihety, that stressed freedom. And not just freedom, but freedom of a liberal color such as has been claimed to have evolved only in Western society over the past three hundred years.

References

Althabe, Gerard
    1969 *Oppression et Libération dans l'Imaginaire: Les Communautés Vil-lageoises de la Côte de Madagascar.* Paris: François Maspero.
Asad, Talal
    1979 Equality in Nomadic Social Systems? Notes towards the Dissolution of an Anthropological Category. In *Pastoral Production and Society.* Cambridge: Cambridge University Press.
Barth, Fredrik
    1961 *Nomads of South Persia.* Boston: Little, Brown.
Beattie, John
    1970 On Understanding Ritual. In *Rationality,* edited by Bryan Wilson. Oxford: Basil Blackwell.
Berger, Peter
    1986 *The Capitalist Revolution.* New York: Basic Books.
Berlin, Isaiah
    1969 *Four Essays on Liberty.* Oxford: Oxford University Press.
Birkeli, E.
    1926 *Marques de Boeufs et Traditions de Race. Documents sur l'Ethno-graphie de la Côte Occidentale de Madagascar.* Oslo: Ethnografisk Museum, Bulletin 2.
Bloch, Maurice
    1971 *Placing the Dead.* London: Seminar Press.
    1975 Property and the End of Affinity. In *Marxist Analyses and Social Anthropology,* edited by M. Bloch. London: Tavistock.
    1986 *From Blessing to Violence: History and Ideology in the Circumcision Ritual of the Merina of Madagascar.* Cambridge: Cambridge University Press.
Buxton, Jean
    1958 The Mandari of Southern Sudan. In *Tribes without Rulers,* edited by J. Middleton and D. Tait. London: Routledge and Kegan Paul.
Collingwood, R. G.
    1978 *An Autobiography.* Oxford: Oxford University Press.
Day, J. P.
    1987 *Liberty and Justice.* London: Croom Helm.

171

Deschamps, Hubert
    1961 *Histoire de Madagascar.* Paris: Berger Levrault.
Eggert, Karl
    1986 Mahafaly as a Misnomer. In *Madagascar: Society and History,* edited
        by C. Kottak, J.-A. Rakotoarisoa, A. Southall, and P. Vérin. Dur-
        ham: Carolina Academic Press.
Evans-Pritchard, E. E.
    1940 *The Nuer.* Oxford: Clarendon Press.
Feeley-Harnik, Gillian
    1978 Divine Kingship and the Meaning of History among the Sakalava of
        Madagascar. *Man* n.s., 13:402–17.
    1982 The King's Men in Madagascar: Slavery, Citizenship and Sakalava
        Monarchy. *Africa* 52:31–50.
    1984 The Political Economy of Death: Communication and Change in
        Malagasy Colonial History. *American Ethnologist* 11 (1):1–19.
    1986 Ritual and Work in Madagascar. In *Madagascar: Society and History,*
        edited by C. Kottak, J.-A. Rakotoarisoa, A. Southall, and P. Vérin.
        Durham: Carolina Academic Press.
    1991 *A Green Estate: Restoring Independence in Madagascar.* Washington
        and London: Smithsonian Institution Press.
Giddens, Anthony
    1984 *The Constitution of Society: Outline of a Theory of Structuration.*
        Cambridge: Polity Press.
Goldschmidt, Walter
    1979 A General Model for Pastoral Social Systems. In *Pastoral Production
        and Society.* Cambridge: Cambridge University Press.
Grandidier, A. and G.
    1908 *Histoire de Madagascar.* Vol. 4, *Ethnographie de Madagascar.* Tome
        1. Paris: Imprimerie Nationale.
Grandidier, G., and Decary, R.
    1958 *Histoire de Madagascar.* Vol. 5, *Histoire Politique et Coloniale.* Tome
        3, Fascicule 1. Tananarive: Imprimerie Nationale.
Gulliver, P.
    [1955] 1972 *The Family Herds.* London: Routledge and Kegan Paul.
Haaland, Gunnar
    1969 Economic Determinants in Ethnic Processes. In *Ethnic Groups and
        Boundaries,* edited by Fredrik Barth. Boston: Little, Brown.
Hayek, F. von
    [1960] 1976 *The Constitution of Liberty.* London: Routledge and Kegan
        Paul.
Hirschmann, A. O.
    1970 *Exit, Voice and Loyalty.* Cambridge, Mass.: Harvard University
        Press.
Huntingford, G. W. B.
    1953 *The Nandi of Kenya: Tribal Control in a Pastoral Society.* London:
        Routledge and Kegan Paul.

Huntington, R., and Metcalf, P.
    1979 *Celebrations of Death: The Anthropology of Mortuary Ritual.* Cambridge: Cambridge University Press.
Kent, Raymond
    1970 *Early Kingdoms in Madagascar, 1500–1700.* New York: Holt, Rinehart and Winston.
Kottak, Conrad
    1980 *The Past in the Present: History, Ecology and Cultural Variation in Highland Madagascar.* Ann Arbor: University of Michigan Press.
Locke, John
    [1690] 1952 *An Essay Concerning the True and Original Extent and End of Civil Government.* Chicago: Encyclopedia Britannica.
Magnes, Bernard
    1953 Institutions et Coutumes des Tsimihety. *Bulletin Academie Malgache* 89.
Manners, Robert
    1964 Colonial and Native Land Tenure: A Case Study in Ordained Accommodation. In *Process and Pattern in Culture: Essays in Honour of Julian Steward,* edited by R. A. Manners. Chicago: Aldine Publishing.
Mannoni, O.
    1956 *Prospero and Caliban: The Psychology of Colonialism.* New York: Praeger.
Marcus, George
    1980 Rhetoric and the Ethnographic Genre in Anthropological Research. *Current Anthropology* 21:507–10.
Marcus, George, and Cushman, D.
    1982 Ethnographies as Texts. In *Annual Review of Anthropology.* Stanford: Annual Reviews.
Mill, J. S.
    [1861] 1952 *Representative Government.* Chicago: Encyclopedia Britannica.
Molet, Louis
    1953 *Le Boeuf dans l'Ankaizinana: Son Importance Sociale et Economique.* Mémoires de l'Institut Scientifique de Madagascar, Serie C. Tome 2. Tananarive.
    1956 *Démographie de l'Ankaizinana.* Mémoires de l'Institut Scientifique de Madagascar, Serie C. Tome 3. Tananarive.
    1959 *L'Expansion Tsimihety.* Mémoires de l'Institut Scientifique de Madagascar, Serie C. Tome 5. Tananarive.
Nozick, Robert
    1974 *Anarchy, State, and Utopia.* New York: Basic Books.
Polanyi, Michael
    1966 *The Tacit Dimension.* New York: Doubleday.
Raz, Joseph
    1986 *The Morality of Freedom.* Oxford: Clarendon Press.

Southall, Aidan
    1986 Common Themes in Malagasy Culture. In *Madagascar: Society and History,* edited by C. Kottak, J.-A. Rakotoarisoa, A. Southall, and P. Vérin. Durham: Carolina Academic Press.
Thompson, V., and Adloff, R.
    1965 *The Malagasy Republic.* Stanford: Stanford University Press.
Wilson, Peter J.
    1967 Tsimihety Kinship and Descent. *Africa* 35:133–54.
    1971 Sentimental Structure: Migration and Descent among the Tsimihety. *American Anthropologist* 73:193–208.
    1977 The Problem with Primitive Folk. *Natural History* 81 (10):26.

Index

Aesthetics: and cattle 74, 76–80; lack of, 42, 71

Aggression, lack of, 162

Ambenilahy (co-resident brothers), 105; and allocation of land, 106; as co-heads of village, 106; as tomb guardians, 106

Androna: confines of, 163; defined, 37; isolation of, 35; original population (Vohilava), 43; settlement of, 34–35; as sphere of influence, 44; topography, 36, 38

Antandrona, loose association, 20

Anthropologist: as outsider, 8; as political problem, 3; as a political status, 8

Asareky (work group), 69; varied composition of, 69

Avoidance, as political tactic, 60

Barter, 67; of salt, honey, tobacco, 89

Benyowski, Count de, 18

Burial: described, 129; feasting, 130; females loosen hair at, 131; funeral procession, 130; imperativeness and formality of, 120; mourning not directed at, 131; personal goods accompany corpse, 131; special binding and wrapping of corpse, 130

Cash economy, excluded, 67

Cattle: anthropologist's misunderstanding of, 72; byres, 74; collec-

tively grazed, individually owned, 53; distribution, 80; earmarks, 93–95; as focus of identity, 84; herd building, 80; importance of horns, 77; and inequality, 81–82, 91; little commercial importance, 73; nonutilitarian, 75–76, 82, 160; offering of, 81; ownership universal, 82; as part of closed system, 91, 93; preoccupation with, 75; and prestige, 76, 81, 82; rough statistics about, 73; rustling, 84–87; small contribution to subsistence, 73, 84; as source of aesthetics, 72, 76–80, 92; and supernatural, 92–93; as toys, 92; Tsimihety attachment to, 72; as wealth, 91

Circumcision (*mamora zaza*): by invitation, 114; many Tsimihety uncircumcised, 114; more formalized occasions of, 114; no ritual for, 114; optional, 115; role of mother's brother in, 114; unplanned, 113

Civil war, in nineteenth century, 19

Colonization: commercial motives, 27; failure of commerce, 28; by French, xi, 22; French policy, 26; protests against, 23

Conservatism, 168; and rejection of modernization, 168

Constraint, ix, 33

Contact, ix; as context, x, 8, 9; as contrast, x

Crafts, minimal production of, 88–89

175

DATE DUE

JUL 1 4 1998			
MAY 0 6 1999			
			Printed in USA